Tell Me the Stories of Jesus

Tell Me the Stories of Jesus

A companion to the remembered gospel

Janet Lees

WILD GOOSE PUBLICATIONS

Copyright © Janet Lees 2011

Published 2011 by
Wild Goose Publications
4th Floor, Savoy House, 140 Sauchiehall St, Glasgow G2 3DH, UK
www.ionabooks.com
Wild Goose Publications is the publishing division
of the Iona Community.
Scottish Charity No. SC003794. Limited Company Reg. No. SC096243.

ISBN 978-1-84952-187-1

The publishers gratefully acknowledge the support of the Drummond
Trust, 3 Pitt Terrace, Stirling FK8 2EY in producing this book.

A catalogue record for this book is available
from the British Library.

Overseas distribution
Australia: Willow Connection Pty Ltd, Unit 4A, 3-9 Kenneth Road,
Manly Vale, NSW 2093
New Zealand: Pleroma, Higginson Street, Otane 4170,
Central Hawkes Bay
Canada: Novalis/Bayard Publishing & Distribution,
10 Lower Spadina Ave., Suite 400, Toronto, Ontario M5V 2Z2

Printed by Bell & Bain, Thornliebank, Glasgow

Mixed Sources
Product group from well-managed
forests and other controlled sources
www.fsc.org Cert no. TT-COC-002769
© 1996 Forest Stewardship Council
FSC

Contents

Acknowledgements

I am grateful to all those who have been interested in developing the 'remembered Bible' methodology that is described in this book. I do not claim it as my own, only that I enjoy using it and having tried to do so consistently and systematically have also described here the fruits of some of those labours. The work has taken place in various parts of Britain, mostly in United Reformed Churches, and frequently within the Yorkshire Synod of that denomination. My thanks to all those who agreed to their real examples being included. Thanks to the Huddersfield TLS group, especially Angela, Jo and Penny, who encouraged me a lot. Thanks to Jane Stranz and Gwen Smithies who have helped to midwife this book. Thanks to Bob Warwicker who copes with all computer related questions and to Hannah Warwicker who has lived RB for most of her life and now does it alongside me in ways that are encouraging, entertaining and revelatory.

Preface

Tell me the stories of Jesus I love to hear;
Things I would ask Him to tell me if He were here;
Scenes by the wayside, tales of the sea,
Stories of Jesus, tell them to me.

William H Parker

In a discussion with four other adults studying the gospels, we reviewed the Bible commentaries we were each using, who had written them and whether or not we would recommend them to others in the group. As we talked it struck me that none of the commentaries in common use were by women. Of course, there are commentaries by women (go on, name some) but most seem to be by men. I voiced this observation aloud: 'What, no women then?' We giggled together and I added, sotto voce, 'Note to self, write gospel commentary by next week.' This, then, was the place where this book started.

It had other preliminary threads like *Word of Mouth*, my first book about the remembered Bible published by Wild Goose in 2007. That book was the fruit of several years' work on using the remembered Bible with two small churches in north-east Sheffield. In some ways this present book is what came next, when the method was used in lots of other places and with lots of other people.

So what sort of companion to the gospel might a book about the remembered Bible be? Unlike a commentary on the written gospels – any one or more of them – it will not be about chapters and verses. Although some folk remember the Bible in chapters and verses, most people I have worked with do not seem to. They remember in narrative or story, the beginnings and ends of which are not usually marked by divisions into chapters and verses as found in the written gospels. Nor will this book be about the meanings of Greek words, or how this sounds in Aramaic, or what that punctuation adds. Occasionally when remembering the Bible ordinary people add thoughts about specific translations that they have heard of, but most do not. Sometimes a whole word or phrase will be remembered from a particular well loved translation, but, as I will say again later, remembering the Bible is not about rote repetition. Most ordinary people remember in their own language, in whatever form that takes.

Rather, this companion to the remembered gospel will be about the why, how, when, where and what of the gospel and remembering it in community. It will include some real-life examples of remembering and some ways of doing remembering in particular contexts to enhance community-building in different ways. It will lead up to the Remembered One: Jesus, the Life Giver whose gospel it is. It also includes examples of prayers and reflections that have grown out of RB. I hope it will answer some frequently asked questions about remembering the Bible but I also hope it will provide further inspiration to 'just go for it'.

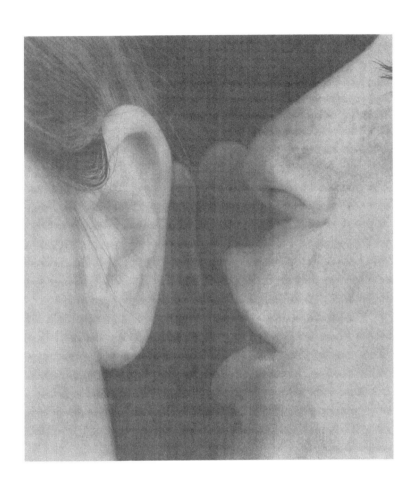

Chapter one

Remembering why

Remembering why

First let me hear how the children stood round His knee,
And I shall fancy His blessing resting on me;
Words full of kindness, deeds full of grace,
All in the love light of Jesus' face.
William H Parker

The purpose of the gospel is to change things. We have this good news to share in order that we, individuals and communities, might be transformed. The change the gospel offers is from death to life. If we choose to respond to the life-giving story of Jesus, we are on the road to life. I hope that this resource book will be a good companion to our remembering of the gospel, and that it will help change both individuals and communities in our travels on the road to life.

'We did the woman at the well last year,' said a group of folk with whom I had been invited to work on remembering the Bible (RB). What exactly they 'did' to the woman at the well those twelve months before I'm not exactly sure, but the phrase – or a variation on it – is not uncommon in dead churches. 'We've done it before' is usually accompanied by a dreary apathy. It often has an echo: if we've done it before, 'therefore we know that' and in knowing it don't need to revisit it.

Given the limited number of chapters in the written gospels and the limited number of books in the closed canon of Christian scripture as a whole, it seems to me that – outside a few obscure bits, the relevance of which seems to escape even the most hardy biblical scholars – it is highly likely that we will, to some extent, have done it before.

But that is the vital and life-affirming starting point for RB. RB is a can-do process precisely because we have done it before. It is the memories we have of the last time, and the time before that, and all the other times, that contribute to the success of RB. Of course there's always someone who says, usually about now, 'Well, that won't work then: what about all those people who have not heard it before?' This group of people is so often referred to by sceptics in RB sessions that I imagine our ordinary churches bursting to over-flowing with new people who flock in week by week who have never before heard the gospel. Yes, there are some, and we will return to consider this particular case, but it is precisely because it is not the general situation that RB can be a lifeline to churches now.

This book is for anyone who is enthusiastic about the gospel – the good news – of Jesus Christ. If you also like to be creative and have fun, that will help too. It's likely that you can catch or generate that creative, fun spirit if you start using RB with a group of folk who are willing to 'just go for it'.

The question behind this book is: *How can oral/remembered versions of the Bible be used today to transmit the story of Jesus, the Life Giver?*

Most people who read books about Jesus are probably familiar with a written collection of stories about his life in the New Testament, called the gospels. In contemporary Western culture the written word has a lot of power. The power attributed to the written versions of the gospels is a product of a long process stretching over two millennia. Part of that process is the role played by word of mouth or oral transmission. If the written words are somehow linked to the life and teaching of a first-century Middle-Eastern person called Jesus of Nazareth, how did they get into print? There are bits of that process about which we can be certain. We have the illumi-nated manuscripts of the Middle Ages, the early attempts to print the Bible in Europe and, yes, we have some very old bits of papyrus in archaic languages. We also have lots of different printed versions of the Bible in global contemporary languages. Those are just some facts about the written Bible.

But the written Bible would not exist without an oral/remem-bered Bible alongside it. In the first place, we have no evidence that Jesus of Nazareth himself wrote down anything he said, and if he did, it does not appear to have survived to the present day. It seems likely that in the tradition of his forebears he was an oral teacher. This way of teaching was common in his culture and his time but it is also common today in cultures around the world that are not dominated by literacy. Even in literate cultures, oral and written teaching go hand in hand. There is a gap between the words Jesus spoke as an oral teacher and the first written versions of his life and teaching that survive. That gap has been the concern of scholarship and speculation for over a century now, but it is not the primary concern of this book. I only mention this gap here because in this book we will be dealing in such gaps, and from time to time the relationship between oral and written versions of the gospels.

Gerald West says that African interpreters of the Bible use both written and remembered/oral versions of the text (West, 1999). Both versions of the Bible are also available to people in the developed nations today. However, in the church – the self-appointed keeper of the gospel – the written version dominates and has been given greater authority than the remembered/oral version. This is a question of control. The written version of the Bible may exist in several different forms (we call them translations) but having a written version at all means that the church can control access to it: who uses it and how it is used.

Oral versions are much more varied and less easy to control. Of course, they can be controlled by undermining the confidence and authority of the tellers, for example. But it is difficult to stop people telling stories or ultimately to control the stories they tell. Thus remembered/oral versions of the Bible are potentially more subversive than written ones. That is not to say that all remembered/oral versions are like this. As we shall see, remembered/oral versions can also be conformist, narrow and deathly. In order to remember and tell the story of Jesus the Life Giver, these are some of the tendencies we will need to counter.

But why worry about remembered/oral versions of the gospels at all in this day and age? The answer is because they are there. Out there, in the world of faith and doubt, belief and unbelief – in other words, the real world – remembered/oral versions of the gospels are circulating. For some people it is remembered/oral versions that are their primary point of access to the Bible. For others, who may also have access to written versions, the remembered/oral versions are still important, a version of choice and a creative way to engage with the story of the Life Giver.

Let me say something about different groups of people. Remembered Bible/oral gospel users come in many and various shapes and sizes, with different backgrounds and experiences, some of which are more marginalised than others. One group consists of those who have no access to written Bibles because they do not read. These people may have communication difficulties of various kinds that limit access to reading and writing. The group could include people with learning and communication impairments, although it will not include all such people, some of whom may fall into the next two groups. Others are pre-readers who will one day probably read but do not do so yet, usually on the grounds of age, opportunity and so on. There are others who are scant readers. This latter group read a bit but it is not their preferred activity due to lack of opportunity, confidence and so on. Of course, there may be other readers of the Bible who decide to read less and remember more in order to better appreciate the role of remembered/oral versions in the transmission of the gospel and to get alongside folk who prefer to use these methods. I would place myself in this latter group.

I choose to use the remembered Bible and oral versions of the gospel although I can and do use printed versions. I do this because as a speech therapist I work alongside people with learning and communication impairments who use remembered/oral versions. I also work with pre-readers and scant readers. All of these are ordinary people who interpret the story of the Life Giver in their daily lives. It is because I am interested in how they do this, and how we can do it together, that I have been developing a process I call Remembering the Bible (or RB) for some 15 years now. The process as I have practised it has concentrated on the story of Jesus' life and ministry, the gospel, and what it means to the ordinary people who remember it.

This book is a continuation of that work. It has been informed by the lived experiences of ordinary remembered Bible and oral gospel users from local communities and by scholarship from several different disciplines including biblical studies, disability studies, sociology and human communication studies to name a few.

Remembering what

Consider this situation: I'm doing some RB at a church I've visited before.[1] There are 14 adults present on comfy chairs in a sort of semicircle and they range in age from 50 to 90 years old. I begin by asking, 'Do you remember Jesus praying with his disciples?' I often begin with a broad subject like this to get people talking to each other. Alice, in the front row, about 90 years old, says firmly, 'No.' Now I happen to know Alice and that she has been coming to church almost all of her life and has a remembered Bible in her. At this point I have to decide what approach to take. Is it enough to accept that Alice says no she doesn't remember Jesus praying with his disciples or do I follow my hunch that this is not true? In other words, I think Alice does remember that Jesus prayed with his disciples but I can't for the life of me think why she has denied it. So I go up to Alice, kneel down in front of her and taking her hands in mine look her fully in the face and say again, 'Alice, do you remember Jesus praying with his disciples?' And she says, 'Oh, yes of course I do, but I don't remember the details.' So I say: 'That's fine, we'll help each other to remember the details' – and we did.

Alice did remember Jesus praying with his disciples but she said no, either because:

- she didn't remember the details and thought she might be asked to do so if she said yes;
- she didn't clearly hear or understand my first question when addressed to the whole group and so said no to what she thought I said. When I repeated the question to her alone she heard and understood it;
- it seemed easier to say no and avoid getting into a more complex situation that she didn't feel she could cope with;
- a combination of these things;
- something else.

It is not unusual in our ageing churches in which passivity has become a common feature of adult behaviour to find that people say they can't remember. Of course, some people can't remember and it is important not to mix the two up. Being put on the spot about remembering can feel uncomfortable. A sense of failure is a sure way to turn adults off learning together. In a small group like the one described and with which the facilitator is familiar it may be possible to deal with the situation more creatively as in the above example. But how can we help adults to see that they can remember things together? Try this activity that I call 'Remembering the Cellist of Sarajevo'. It is not about the Bible, which can help people who think that might be a bit difficult.

An activity to help people begin remembering

This story has been told many times since the siege of Sarajevo which lasted from 1992 to 1996 during the Balkan war. As such there are many versions of the story and it is an example of oral history. Tell the story to the group and say you will ask them about it again later. There's no need to tell the story word for word. Tell it in your own words and in your own way.

The story goes like this …

> *In the city of Sarajevo there was to be a concert by a famous string quartet. They had come to play there to demonstrate that the world had not forgotten Sarajevo. The morning after the concert the cello player did an extraordinary thing. He took his cello out into the square at midday and sat down to play. He played for several minutes. Then some soldiers came rushing into the square. They surrounded the cellist and shouted at him, 'Stop! Stop!' 'What are you doing!' 'You cannot do that here,' and so on, all trying to stop the cellist from playing. The cellist continued to play until the end of the music. The soldiers berated him again saying, 'Don't you know this is a dangerous place?' 'Can't you see what is happening here?' The cellist turned to them and said, 'Can't you*

see what is happening here?'

The next day at midday the cellist came out into the square again and played in the same way. He did this every day at midday for one month. Ask yourself the question, 'Can you see what is happening here?'

It is highly possible that participants will have heard a version of the story before. Like all good stories there are many versions. It may evoke some comments about 'knowing a different version' or 'what happened next?' Leave these questions and comments for a short time. If possible do something else instead (have a bun, introduce a song, anything!). Then after a while ask the group to remember the story of the cellist in small groups. Ask each group to retell their version of the story to the whole group. The purpose of this is to demonstrate two things: we are able to remember and it is highly likely that we will have remembered differently. It also helps us to learn to listen to each other's rememberings.

If you have time and it seems helpful, go back to the questions and comments about the story and see if a short discussion of some of these points can help the group to understand who remembered what and how oral stories work differently from printed ones.

Remembering the gospel and prayer

It is good practice to begin and/or end RB sessions with prayer. These prayers can be of any style or tradition but ones which build on RB can help us to see the connections within our faith between the Bible and prayer. Here are two examples linking to RB of variations on traditional and well known prayers: the prayer of St Francis and the prayer which is called St Patrick's Breastplate.

Remembering, after St Francis[2]

Make me a channel of your peace:
    where there is chaos,
    may patterns emerge;
    where there are words,
    sentences take shape;
    where there are fragments,
    stories unfold.

For it is in remembering that we forget,
in forgiving that we are released to forgive,
and in listening that we are empowered to speak;
in fighting that we discover our need of peace,
in hugging that we gain courage to let go,
and in creating that we set free the stuff of life.

St Patrick's T-shirt[3]

I'll write it here, the Trinity
The three in one, the one in three.

I recall God's created wonders,
All around me air, earth, fire, water;
And forgiveness for our blunders,
Misuse or pollution of the same.
I recall the Spirit's action,
Interpreting and then translating
Languages of every faction:
Dancing with diversity.

I'll write it here, the Trinity
The three in one, the one in three.

I remember Jesus born in a stable,
Baptised in the river Jordan,
Broke bread, shared wine around a table,
Died on a cross and then rose up,
Appeared to friends, the stuff of fable,
Ate again the 'not last supper',
Left his footprints for us to follow
and celebrate in joy and sorrow.

I'll write it here, the Trinity
The three in one, the one in three.

With me – Christ!
In me – Christ!
Behind me – Christ!
Before me – Christ!
Beside me – Christ!
Beneath me – Christ!
Above me – Christ!
Winning and restoring Christ,
Quiet and confirming Christ,
In heart – Christ!
In mouth – Christ!

I'll write it here, the Trinity
The three in one, the one in three,
Always here, upon my chest,
In remembering this, my life is blessed.

NOTES

[1] This is a real incident but Alice is not this person's real name.
[2] After the Vision4life Day in Blackburn, 28.03.2009.
[3] A version of St Patrick's Breastplate, 15.03.2009.

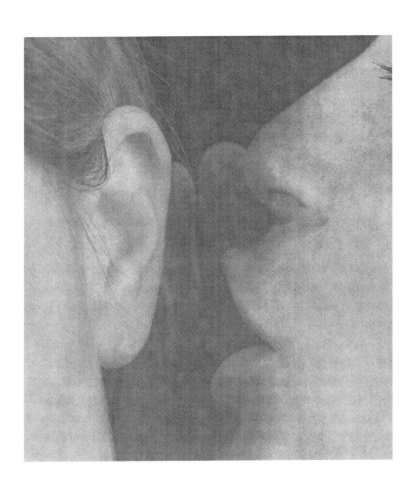

Chapter two

Remembering how

Remembering how

Tell me the story of Jesus,
Write on my heart every word.
Tell me the story most precious,
Sweetest that ever was heard.

Fanny Crosby

Using 'Remembering the Bible' for the first time

'It didn't go very well. They didn't say very much and there were lots of silences. I wasn't sure if I was doing it right.'

This sort of comment is not unusual from someone trying to facilitate the Remembering the Bible (RB) process for the first time. It requires a bit of unpicking to understand what might have been going on.

It didn't go very well
From this example we don't know for sure who thought this. It seems likely the facilitator is speaking of his or her own perceptions. It is possible they got some feedback from the group but if the group was an ordinary congregation who had never done RB before, it is unlikely. Ordinary people are not very experienced at giving constructive feedback. In churches the feedback is often restricted to 'that was a nice service' or variants. This lack of constructive feedback affects facilitators differently, but almost always it feeds into diminishing confidence rather than increasing it. It's not too surprising: if people say nothing, always assume the worst.

'It didn't go very well' might be quite a mild assessment, and might at first sight seem neutral. It says something about expectations: RB is not going to solve all your group participation, learning and empowerment issues in one go. Think back to your first attempts at anything else reasonably complex: no one learns to drive, use a computer or swim the Channel on the first attempt. Keep at it.

They didn't say very much and there were lots of silences
These comments seem to refer to the group participants. Any group of people, even ones who know each other quite well, might not say very much when invited to do RB for the first time or with a new facilitator. Participation requires some confidence on the part of the participants as well as the facilitator. Even if the facilitator has clearly explained the process, the group may still take some time to 'warm up'. Small breakout or gossip groups can help get the voices going. Position is also very important. Where people are sitting at a distance from each other, or there are large amounts of empty space between the facilitator and the group (both things quite common in large, mostly empty churches), the setting itself can be intimidating and silencing. Most of the group may not have experienced hearing their voices in this space. Encourage them by asking them to move closer to each other and moving closer to them. If they seem reluctant to do this, try passing round some biscuits or fruit as an incentive.

The observation that there were lots of silences is important. Silence is not, as I will probably say more than once, a waste of time. There will be silences. They are important. There is no need to fill up every silence with the same voice or voices. Try to live with the silence a bit, even if you or the group are not used to it. Just because people don't speak doesn't mean they aren't thinking about it. Thinking about it may turn into speech later or on another occasion. But even if it doesn't, silence is also valuable.

On not expecting people to keep quiet all of the time
Each RB session has its own blend of chaos and solemnity. In some cultures silence is not the norm for adults, let alone children. Why should it be all hushed up? If you have not seen each other for a while, then it can be a good idea to talk to each other during the session. Without doubt, surprising noise-free moments will appear spontaneously during the course of doing the RB. These are usually much more authentic than the false silence produced by much shushing which says people are not comfortable here.

I wasn't sure if I was doing it right

There is no blueprint for RB. It is not a process that is set in stone. Therefore one cannot do it right or wrong. RB is just something you do like you do. If that sounds woolly and potentially chaotic, it is. We will all do it a bit differently depending on our personality, the characteristics of the group, relationships between group and facilitator, what we're remembering and why. RB is something a group of people in a place do together to get to grips with the transforming effect of the Bible in their community.

However, it is not unusual for first-time facilitators or groups to think they aren't doing it right. The culture of church and society means that failure is not a comfortable option. If it doesn't seem to go with a swing and be hugely successful from the first, it must be wrong. If we're not doing it right, best stop then and go back to what we know. Actually, you are doing it right simply because you are doing it. Keep at it.

So to summarise, RB is something

- you need to just go for
- you need to just go for more than once
- you need the group's co-operation for
- you all need to consider how to make successful – small groups, seating layout, etc
- that contains as many silences as words.

Living God,
stir us up as we remember together,
listening to you and each other
and energise us in words and silence
to be your people in the world.

Tea taker

Here is one way of getting started with RB. It uses what appears to be a well known incident from the gospels as its starting point: Jesus going to tea with Zacchaeus. The activity is done in small informal groups.

There are several incidents in the gospels where Jesus visits someone's home and receives hospitality there. Amongst those most remembered are visits to Martha, Mary and Lazarus, and to Zacchaeus. The Zacchaeus story can be a good remembering activity for people of all ages. It is a good story to use when thinking about issues of welcome and hospitality. Sometimes it can help start a group off if you present some rememberings from other groups. Here are four different rememberings about Zacchaeus.[4]

Put each one on a different card, divide the participants into small groups and give one card to each small group as a way of starting the remembering process. A group may choose to begin with the ideas presented on the card or the card may prompt memories of something else important about the story. Either way it makes it clear that we can do remembering together and we gain insights from the rememberings of others.

Zacchaeus: the short tax collector who climbed a tree.
Jesus invited himself for tea.
Zacchaeus said, 'If I have cheated anyone of anything …'

Zacchaeus, a tax collector, climbed a tree.
He promised to make good any cheating he'd done.
He would only give back money if he had taken it unfairly.

Zacchaeus, a tax collector.
Small in stature, he had to climb a sycamore tree to see Jesus.
He was hated because he was collecting taxes for Rome.
He took more money than he should.
Jesus said he wished to eat with him at his house.
He offered to give money and more back.

Zacchaeus: the tax collector who pays back four times what he took: short in stature but measures up in the end.

This way of beginning to do RB can be used with any story, or with any of the more than 50 starters in the last chapter of this book. It's best to begin with stories that frequently feature in shared remember-ings of the gospel, to give people confidence that they can do it; but using other people's rememberings to start off a group remembering can be one way of introducing a less well remembered episode.

Tea taker,
we welcome you
as you welcome us.
It will cost you dearly
but so are we dearly loved.

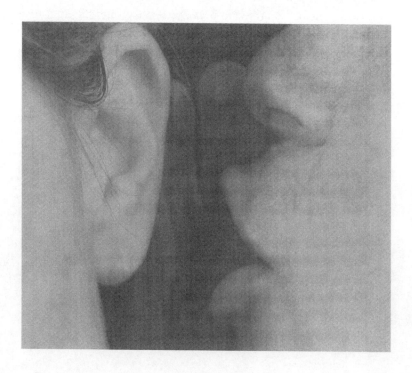

Forgiveness is ...

We make a mistake,
you rub it out.

We fall short,
you build us up.

We get it wrong,
you help us put it right.

We feel bogged down,
you dig us out.

We overlook an opportunity,
you offer us another new start.

We are consumed with trying to impress,
you accept us as we are.

We cheat our neighbours,
you invite us to tea.

FAQs about RB

This section arises from the questions I am often asked about using
RB. Such questions usually have two main foci: what to do when
people get it wrong and how RB can be done with people who don't
know the Bible. It is interesting that these two issues are about why
RB can't or won't work, either because it will encourage people to use
the Bible erroneously or because it will exclude all those people who
have not yet heard the story of Jesus. It is not unusual for the 'we can't
do it' or 'it can't be done' message to be passed on in churches. I have
frequently been told this, and not just about RB. However, we need
to be clear that such messages are not the hallmark of Christian leadership, which is a Spirit-empowered, Jesus-accompanied, Creator-graced
activity that is characterised by a 'can-do' approach.

Nonetheless, it is important to take genuine concerns seriously, and so here are some responses to the most frequently asked questions about RB.

'We don't know 'owt about Bible'
This was the first response of six teenage boys aged 14-16 from a housing estate in West Yorkshire.[5] Using a piece of string to map out Jesus' life from his birth to his death and resurrection[6] over a period of forty-five minutes, they remembered several things. First off, things around his childhood:

- his birth, 'in a what do you call it';
- 'killing all them babies less than two year old', because the king was jealous and afraid;
- where did he go to then? Did he lie low and for how long?
- getting lost in a temple when he was 12 years old

This was followed by three things in the middle of his adult life:
- going into the desert for forty days and forty nights when he lived in a cave near a mountain, and he had to find stuff to drink and eat;
- with some fishermen, telling them to put their nets down on this side of the boat and they pulled it in and it was full of fish (this one accompanied by miming and acting);
- going into Jerusalem on a donkey.

Then for Holy Week we had

- the Last Supper: he was with his friends, they had bread and wine and he said it was his body and his blood;
- his death;
- then he came alive again a few days later;
- after he came back to life he had another supper with some friends so that was the 'not last supper' then, wasn't it?

With patient persistence these boys were able to see that they did have a Bible in them and this became the foundation of a series of sessions using RB, particularly around the Holy Week narrative, exploring who Jesus was. We used their language as much as possible and took our time.

What happens when the [Bible] story gets changed in the retelling?
One of the most frequently asked questions about RB is: 'What if they do it wrong?' At the heart of this question is a concern for authority, not just how we interpret the Bible but who is authorised to tell us how to interpret (Perrin, 2007). Consider this story:

> *There was once a woman who was trying to put herself through Bible college, only she didn't have a grant, an inheritance or a salary to help her. In fact she was broke. So, after giving this a lot of prayerful thought, she decided her only option was to 'go on the game' and work as a prostitute to finance her biblical studies …*

Like the story of the cellist in Sarajevo, you might be asking yourself whether this story is true. Well, it was told to me by someone else. And she heard it told by two other people.

In the first retelling, the young woman who had no money decided that she would have to work in a strip club. In the second retelling, the woman with no money had become a prostitute.

I wondered if this is what had happened to Mary Magdalene. Was Mary trying to put herself through Rabbinical College when she met Jesus? Several retellings later and the church had her recast as the archetypal fallen woman, the prostitute that Jesus 'rescues', of which there is no mention in the written gospels. If anything, this example shows how RB and oral versions of the gospel can produce versions that are at the very least unhelpful, and that can, as in this example, be detrimental to gender-equal community-building for centuries.

Even if this didn't happen to Mary, it does give us food for thought:

- What happens when people retell each other's stories?
- What did Jesus make of the disciples' attempts to retell the stories he told them?

- Isn't retelling stories just too full of pitfalls to make it a good way of interpreting the Bible?

As far as the last point is concerned, it depends very much on what the facilitator and group members do when such rememberings are shared. Try to move gently and carefully between contributions. Ask if other group members have any other versions or ideas about the story, or suggest another version or idea that comes from a different group or different activity but which could be a catalyst for the whole group at this point. Try to avoid a strongly negative reaction as this is more likely to inhibit contributions than elicit them.

What if they make the stories up?
'I remember Jesus went round to his granddad's house and he stayed there when he was growing up,' said Nathaniel, aged 3 years.[7]

So is this RB right or wrong?

Well, 'Jesus probably had a granddad,' said the mother of two children and 'I often go to my granddad's house,' said a girl, aged 9 years.

Several recent studies with religious families have confirmed that grandparents are seen as having an important role in a child's development.[8]

It is quite possible, even likely, that Jesus had a granddad. Christian tradition has it that Mary's parents were called Ann and Joachim (according to the Proto-Gospel or Protoevangelion of James). There are a number of other ideas about Mary's parents. For example, the 17th-century painting of them entitled 'The Virgin Mary with her parents' in the collection of the Society of Antiquaries, London offers us a glimpse of what people thought about this family several hundred years ago.

These developments possibly reflect a concern for the stability of family life and that this be reflected in the lives of biblical characters. But if you are three years old it is not wrong to say that Jesus visited his granddad. It is not even wrong if you are thirty-three or one hundred and three. It is founded on personal experience and makes sense in this context. It is an aspect of RB which we do not find in the written

Bible and this is one of the main ways in which the two genres differ.

If we use RB, not only is everyone a biblical interpreter but the issue of authority within the interpreting community is also challenged. If everyone has their own RB and takes possession of that, then everyone has authority to interpret, and it is a shared authority that we are building up, from the bottom, not an imposed authority from the top. Even three-year-olds can be biblical interpreters because it's their remembered Bible they are interpreting. This encourages us all to become active participants in the interpretive process rather than passively waiting for others to interpret for us.

It is generally agreed that the written gospels were assembled over time. They probably contain some original oral sayings attributable to the Jesus of the first century and his followers. These have been selected, edited and reassembled to reflect particular concerns, ideas and theologies. There are more of these texts than the four we have in our printed Bibles. It is possible, even highly likely, that there have been others that are now lost or at least not yet found. At some time in the past some versions of the story of Jesus' life and ministry were thought authoritative and some were not, based on the power struggles going on in the early church. The 'authoritative' ones were promoted and the others were rejected and marginalised. As a result we have the four written gospels included in the Bible today and the picture of Jesus contained in them. The process of collecting, interpreting and giving authority has gone on in different ways since those early days – for example when European missionaries introduced the gospel to other parts of the world in the 18th-20th centuries.

This process is perhaps more obvious when RB is used, but it is not wrong. It is just more transparent. Being willing to use RB signals that the group is ready to share the task of interpretation and build community on the basis of shared authority.

The role of eyewitnesses in the transmission of scripture has always been important. Biblical scholars have looked for clues to eyewitness accounts in the written-down Bible. Similarly there may be members of your group who remember who told a story, even if that person is not now present (moved away, died, etc). But many of the stories will have either become disconnected from the original teller or become hybridised, resulting in multiple ownership, over time. They have in effect become the group's stories.

In these ways, using RB helps us to a renewed understanding of the formation of the written gospels and the link to authority and leadership that this process reveals. When someone asks me, 'What if they get it wrong?' I know that person is likely to give high authority to the printed text in the form in which it is now used by the church. I am much more interested in how ordinary people interpret the stories of the gospel, and how groups and communities use these stories to build up new patterns of ministry and mission.

Once I was co-leading with my daughter Hannah, then 16, an RB session with women in Germany. She speaks German and I do not. I asked her to prompt me if in the course of introducing RB there was something I had missed out. Hannah had been doing RB since she was about five years old. She said to me, 'Tell them about it not being wrong.' I took that to mean I had not said enough about this aspect of the process: that each of us possesses our own RB and that therefore there is no 'wrong'. I also took it to mean that this was one of the aspects Hannah considered important about the process and was something she had internalised over the time she had been doing RB. RB had contributed to making her an active biblical interpreter.

Not remembering

Not remembering is said to be increasing in our society. As our population ages and suffers additional impairments, a significant number of people are losing their memory. We call this condition dementia. So how does RB fit with dementia?

There are many kinds of dementia, by no means all the same. It is not usually a good idea to generalise too much about the capacities of individuals even if they have the same condition. The main things to remember about RB and dementia are:

- RB is a can-do process which works because we do it together;
- it is not about the memory of an individual but about the

shared rememberings of a group or community of people;

- even when we forget some things we may remember others;
- in some forms of dementia, stuff that has been in us for a long time may be easier to remember than recent events.

Do not rule out doing RB with people who forget stuff. Concentrate on developing the right environment for remembering. It needs to feel safe. Having different kinds of 'memory joggers', such as pictures, photographs and objects, can help. Go carefully and remember that silence is not a waste of time.

God in me
A speech therapist rewrites the Sarum Prayer

God be in me and my impairments:
God be in my eyes and in my blindness;
God be in my ears and in my deafness;
God be in my head and in my madness;
God be in my legs and in my lameness;
God be in my hands and in my clumsiness;
God be in my mouth and in my silence;
God be at my end and in my dementing.

NOTES

[4] Huddersfield TLS Group: 30.11.2009.
[5] Thanks to members of Brackenhall Boys' Brigade and their leader Barry Simmons for this opportunity to do RB.
[6] This activity is called 'The Jesus lifeline' and is in *Word of Mouth*, pages 60-61.
[7] Nathaniel is a member of Brackenhall United Reformed Church.
[8] See for example Horwarth et al 2008 and Lees 2009.

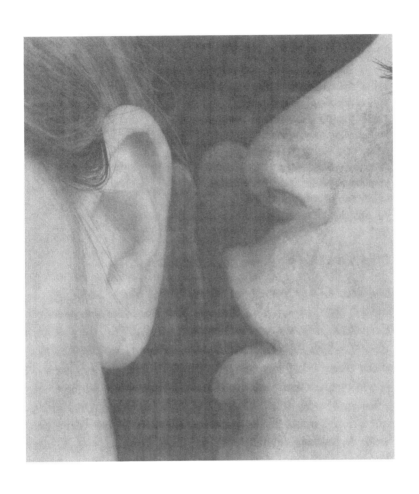

Chapter three

Remembering when

Remembering when

Tell of the cross where they nailed Him,
Writhing in anguish and pain.
Tell of the grave where they laid Him,
Tell how He liveth again.
Love in that story so tender,
Clearer than ever I see.
Stay, let me weep while you whisper,
Love paid the ransom for me.
Fanny Crosby

Crosswards through the cross woods

On Good Friday 2009 about twenty folk of all ages and a few dogs
walked seven or so miles through West Yorkshire countryside to
Castle Hill for a service of worship and witness. They were joined at
the hill, which shows signs of human activity from 4,000 BCE, by
about thirty other less energetic people. Along the way we often
passed through small woodland areas. Just breaking into bud, these
woodlands were small oases of wildlife undergoing the natural
springtime process of regeneration. Blankets of last year's fallen
leaves in hollows; twisted roots and fallen branches; the odd dead
hedgehog; all witness to the life and death of the woods. On this lim-
inal day, as we trod our way through these woodlands, there was a
fresh awareness of the path between life and death. On the hill we
heard the story of the hill far away and the Suffering One. Amongst
those who gathered to listen, some were not associated formally with
any organised Christian fellowship. These are the Good Friday
people of our age, who walk crosswards through woods and up the
hill to remember, and who still count. They are a good example of
the when of remembering the Bible.

It is possible to remember the Bible at any time. However, where
we do it will affect our remembering. If we do it in church, in worship, we are in a particular setting that can shape the way it goes.

Depending on the congregation, this might lead to more or less formality. A service of one hour will put some boundaries on the time available for remembering. If we do it outside or at a different sort of event, then these environments will also influence our RB. We might do more or less RB and perhaps add several rememberings together into a sequence.

Remembering the Passion

The Passion octave, from Palm Sunday to Easter Day, is the core of the gospel whether written or remembered. The last week of Jesus' life can generate some good RB and our annual revisiting of this week we call Holy can provide creative situations for it.

> *'Keeping us hanging on like this. It's like crucifixion. Just not knowing what will happen. It's all drawn out and painful in the extreme.'*

This remark was made not in a church but in a secular workplace.[9]

The person speaking was not 'in the church' as the church itself defines such things. However, he was probably part of the 60-70% of the population that describe themselves as Christian. The meeting was not a Bible study (it was about redundancies) – or was it?

For the two years mentioned here I worked in the regional office in the north of England of a national voluntary organisation that supports disabled people. Although the staff called me 'our office vicar' I was not an industrial missioner or workplace chaplain (although I do know some) and my job was to support families of disabled children.

So, we don't do Bible studies when we are office workers ... or do we?

Several times since the beginning of that year I had heard church leaders assert that the Bible has fallen out of British culture. This view is not new. I have come across it in several denominations at all levels. Although I can see that the place of the Bible in British culture has changed, I do not agree that it is now absent. I believe that the Church fails to recognise ways in which the Bible is still present in our culture and, moreover, fails to respond to or nurture these.

I noted that biblical images and stories were referred to by my fellow workers. These have included the Exodus, Psalm 23, and Paul's conversion on the road to Damascus. Reflecting on this, the top four from the gospels seemed to be:

- Jesus changing water into wine;
- Jesus feeding five thousand people;
- Jesus walking on water;
- the crucifixion.

The first three are commonly referred to as miracles. They represent points in the gospel narrative where the humanity of Jesus is subservient to his divinity. Neither you nor I could literally replicate the events depicted. They take us into the stuff of faith that might be hard for modern minds to accept. Yet these are the ones referred to the most often.

Maybe, if you're working in an organisation that is going downhill fast, and your jobs are on the line and possibly your pensions too – in other words, you are desperate – even the most unlikely two-thousand-year-old resources are best not completely ignored.

Maybe workers in the voluntary sector have a higher expectation of the ethical basis of their organisation. Added to which their motivation or vocation for the work they do may mean they are more likely to come from, or continue to be linked to, a faith background. My fellow workers included Christians (Anglican, Roman Catholic, Salvation Army) and one was a Sikh.

Maybe none of this would happen if there was no 'office vicar'. In discussing that point with others who have a chosen faith stance and who have worked in a variety of offices, staff rooms etc, the general view seemed to be that 'They know who we are' and 'Sometimes they seek us out' or, to put it another way, 'We have our uses.'

The fact that the crucifixion is also commonly mentioned deserves particular attention. After all, this is a key part of the Christian narrative. People have not forgotten that Jesus was crucified. If Paul claims, 'I preach Christ and him crucified,' as his public credentials as a follower of Jesus, then the one who said *Keeping us hanging on like this. It's like crucifixion …* 'was beginning to do the same.

Of course it all depends where it is leading. It depends on what happens next. How do people respond to the biblical references used by others? What do these mean to them?

Would that be a Bible study?

What I notice is that people use these references in different ways. Sometimes they use them to lighten the oppressive feeling of a situation. In a meeting about redundancies (of which we had a few) the references were greeted with smiles and even laughter. The message is that we might feel powerless but don't forget. Stories of hope don't need to be told in full to serve that function. Laughing about the Bible seems therapeutic (although I can imagine many worthy Christian folk who would find it difficult).

In my own situation, the story of the crucifixion was used differently. We felt powerless. We couldn't think of anything we could do that would change the minds of the management. We just felt like we were hanging on to the bitter end. The crucifixion story was mentioned to validate our feelings. We were not alone. Again the story was not told in full but there was clearly enough of a common understanding of it for the reference to work for everyone: here is one who shared our experience.

No one was 'leading' this biblical interpretation in the traditional sense. I certainly said nothing and I don't think it is necessary for the 'office vicar' to speak. If other 'office vicars' are looking to develop a strategy around remembering the Bible at work, I suggest the following:

- listen out for examples of biblical images and stories being used at work;
- note how they are used and why;
- don't be tempted to talk too much;
- use your own remembered Bible when it seems appropriate;
- see what happens next.

> *Christ of the Easter Vigil,*
> *as you hung on for us,*
> *help us to hang on*
> *to and for each other.*
> *Remind us that we all still count,*
> *in that endless crowd of witnesses.*
> *Confirm us as cross people*
> *as we take the steps that lead us*
> *from death to life.*

When someone has died

Three days after my mother died, I was sitting in the garden with my father eating the last bread pudding she had made. As we munched our way through her legendary recipe I asked Dad what from the Bible reminded him of Mum. Without hesitation he named Jesus feeding the multitude and the many baskets of leftovers. My mum was like Jesus: she could feed people and did so in many different circumstances, always making the best use of leftovers. It was this con-nection and the way in which she used it to help build community that we celebrated together.

Remembering you …

Remembering you is like making bread pudding.
I collect the ingredients:
sweet juicy raisins for the good times,
crunchy nuts for the hard ones.
And between them all
the everyday stuff of ordinary life:
the bread we all took so much for granted,
basketfuls of it.
I hope there will always be enough leftovers.

On another occasion I was at Sue's house and she and her family were telling me about Tony, who had just died. Tony was a builder but before that he'd had a garage selling second-hand cars. After they had told me many stories about Tony as they remembered him, I asked them what part of the Bible reminded them of Tony. There was a long silence during which they thought about this. Then Marcus, Tony's son-in-law said, 'Tony reminds me of the Good Samaritan.'

About four hundred people, many from the local building trade, attended the service of thanksgiving for his life. His family chose the story of the Good Samaritan for the service because 'Tony was always helping people'. They told a story of how he had once accepted a very large pumpkin in settlement of an account a customer was unable to pay. When I repeated this story at the service I asked the congregation if any of them thought they could run a business like that? I linked this to the saying about the grain of wheat that only produces more grains if it falls into the ground and dies. One way in which Tony's life would produce more grains was if his fellow builders conducted their businesses just like he had. Can anyone conduct a business like that? Tony did. I remember him every time I see a pumpkin.

Draw us to you,
God of all,
that in our dying
and our living
we may bring
glory and honour
to your name
as we seek to serve you
with integrity. [10]

Getting crafty with RB

Not everyone is a talker or thinker. Some people are doers or makers. Doers or makers like to be more hands-on with their RB. Even talkers and thinkers can benefit from doing or making alongside RB. Here are some tried and tested ideas to get you started using crafts.

Scrapbooking the gospel
Scrapbooking is a popular hobby for which there are now many magazines, websites, courses and speciality craft shops. If you remember buying a simple sugar paper scrapbook and pot of glue for a few pence from your money box and you've not revisited scrapbooking since your childhood, you're in for a surprise when you explore just what can be done now.

Scrapbooking is a way of working with memories by using pictures and photographs with memo-writing or journaling. Usually these are the everyday memories that pepper our lives, from special occasions to our first day at school, but scrapbooking can also be used with RB as a way of exploring and recording – both individually and for a group – just how RB becomes part of our lives together.

An example: scrapbooking the Passion [11]
Invite the group to move into eight similar-sized smaller groups. Give each one a card on which is written one day of the week from Palm Sunday to Easter Day: Palm Sunday; Holy Monday; Holy

Tuesday; Holy Wednesday; Maundy Thursday; Good Friday; Holy Saturday; Easter Day.

Invite each group to spend some time together using RB to remember that day. Some days may be more memorable than others. Some may be busier than others. Invite each group to use scrapbooking materials to record their RB of that day. This can take anything from thirty minutes to two hours depending on the number of people in each group and how much detail they want to record. If scrapbooking supplies are not available, invite each group to make a poster – or for a high tech version perhaps a PowerPoint.

Have a show and tell time to share rememberings with the whole group and retell your own Passion story. When listening to the stories for the whole week remind people not to interrupt. A discussion of what was remembered can take place afterwards if this seems appropriate. Having done this activity several times I can attest to the huge variety of rememberings. For one group of people, Jesus cursed the fig tree on three consecutive days: Monday, Tuesday and Wednesday. No wonder it felt got at! In another group, no one mentioned the fig tree at all on any day.

Make your own cross

For hundreds of years remembered versions of the gospels have been displayed on ancient stone crosses. When they were first erected, some as long ago as the 6th-8th centuries AD, they were the Bibles of their time. Each cross had stories carved on its faces. Most of the oldest crosses in the British Isles today are in the western parts of Scotland and in Ireland. The oldest one on the island of Iona is the St Martin's cross, outside the Abbey.

A project to make your own cross would probably be a communal activity for a small group of people over several weeks or months. If doing this outside, try to make it in the summer. If doing it inside, make sure you have enough room. Whenever and wherever you do it, be sure to think ahead to the health and safety aspects of the project. Of course, if you prefer, you could make your cross on paper rather than on wood, MDF or stone.

Art and RB

Another good starting point for RB is visual art from across cultures and different times. The internet makes it fairly easy to find paintings and drawings of scenes from the gospels from a wide range of sources. If you can't use the internet then a library will have some books on this sort of thing.

In her book *The Other Side of You*, Salley Vickers has her two main characters compare the two paintings of the Supper at Emmaus (also called 'the not last supper' earlier in this book) that were painted by Caravaggio in the 1600s. In the early one, Jesus is shown as a young man in a well lit scene in which people enthusiastically communicate as they eat together. In the later painting there is little light and the sombre scene shows an older, more worn down Jesus, with older companions and a very meagre feast. So which of these is the real supper at Emmaus?

They are a good example of how one person's RB can change over time. Clearly Caravaggio's view of this episode changed over his lifetime. Coming from a culture in which reproducing biblical scenes was a reasonably good way of earning a living as an artist, he painted many others as well – as did numerous artists like him before and since. Around the world today people of different cultures are still depicting the gospel in their own time and place. So why not have a look at some and see what they do for your RB?

Using a PowerPoint projector to show the pictures, or passing postcards around, you can select paintings, photographs or pictures that kick start the RB process or help people to respond with their own pictures, sculptures, etc.

The tomb

From cross to tomb
little is said.
Silence stretches out
as the tomb is sealed.

Prayers for people [12]

In this, the holiest of weeks,
we pray for people:
all the ordinary cross-wise ones,
struggling with the weight of life-changing decisions,
the wait and the agony.
'My God, my God, why have you forsaken me?'
Your haunting cry echoes through us;
our relationships, our hopes and fears.
Cross-bound Christ,
as you hung on for us,
hang on to us now
as we try to embrace each other
with helping and hoping.
With death only a heartbeat away,
may the life you live in us
equip us to face these holy days,
as we move from death to life.

Just this week

Just this week I heard
you were planning to visit
at the end of a long journey,
uncertain what sort of welcome you'd receive.

Just this week I heard
you were struggling to see the way ahead:
good times seemed to be behind,
heaven knows what was round the corner.

Just this week I heard
you were trying to reprioritise:

not everyone seemed to understand
that the time had come to move on.

Just this week I heard
you'd challenged a difficult situation:
trying to remember what sort of body
was meeting round a table.

Just this week I heard
you were standing on the edge of death,
looking into a tomb,
challenged to go on loving.

Just this week it began again:
the week of weeks named holy
when the cost of love breaks in on us,
strips us of everything except
our innate vulnerability.
Weak-wise One,
only your embrace can get us through
just one week.

NOTES

9 An office I worked in from 2004-2006.
10 This prayer first appeared in *Hush the Storm*, the URC Prayer Handbook 2009.
11 You can find more suggestions about scrapbooking the Bible at
   http://www.vision4life.org.uk/index.php/bible-year/desserts/
   bible-scrapbooking/
12 Holy Week 2009, with Barbara and David firmly in mind.

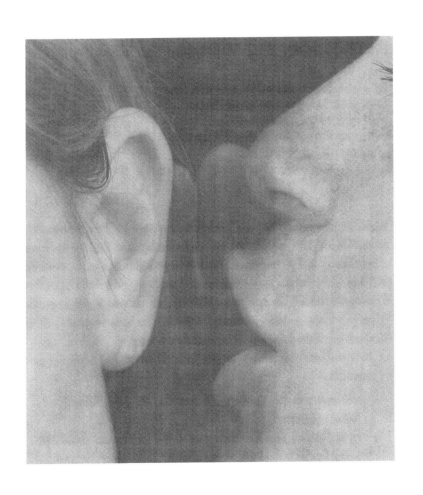

Chapter four

Remembering where

Remembering where

Tell me, in accents of wonder, how rolled the sea,
Tossing the boat in a tempest on Galilee;
And how the Maker, ready and kind,
Chided the billows, and hushed the wind.
William H Parker

Location, location

We don't just remember the Bible when we are in church attending
public worship. Hopefully we use our remembered Bibles a lot more
often than that. Furthermore, it can be a good idea to go to a specific
location with the primary intention of remembering the Bible there.
This could be a 'one off' remembering or part of a series or pilgrimage of remembering around a particular area or place, either
local or one visited for a holiday or other reason.

Remembering the Bible in the Lake District, for example, gave
opportunities to:

- remember stories about the Sea of Galilee, using lakes like
  Windermere;
- go backwards and forwards and round and round these lakes,
  using ferries and roads, remembering Jesus' teaching and
  healing ministry;
- visit graveyards, stone circles and other places of local significance to remember important stories such as the Transfiguration, the Crucifixion and the Resurrection;
- get very wet due to prevailing weather conditions.

Alternatively, remembering the Bible on Iona provided different
opportunities for remembering the same gospel stories or others in a
different setting. In case you are making a pilgrimage to Iona, the
places we chose are given here. Not every group will want to copy
this exactly but it may provide some suggestions for where to start.

Some places to do RB on Iona

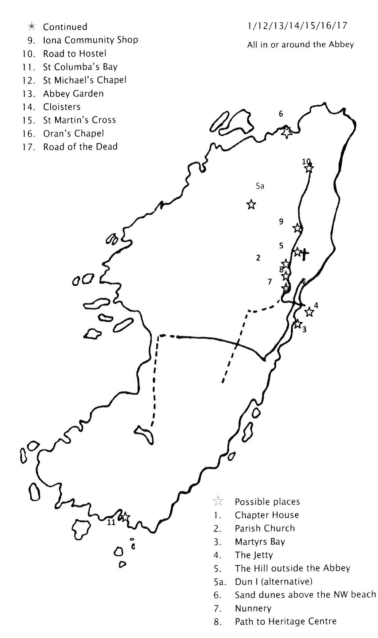

* Continued
9. Iona Community Shop
10. Road to Hostel
11. St Columba's Bay
12. St Michael's Chapel
13. Abbey Garden
14. Cloisters
15. St Martin's Cross
16. Oran's Chapel
17. Road of the Dead

1/12/13/14/15/16/17

All in or around the Abbey

☆ Possible places
1.   Chapter House
2.   Parish Church
3.   Martyrs Bay
4.   The Jetty
5.   The Hill outside the Abbey
5a. Dun I (alternative)
6.   Sand dunes above the NW beach
7.   Nunnery
8.   Path to Heritage Centre

Day	Activity	Venue	Number
1	Read through	Chapter House	1
2	Synagogue in Nazareth	Parish Church	2
2	Jesus teaches from a boat	Martyrs Bay	3
2	The End Times	The Jetty	4
3	Transfiguration	Dun I or Hill by Abbey	5 or 5a
3	The 'lost' parables	Above NW beach	6
4	Centurion's Servant	The village street	7
4	Widow stories	Nunnery	8
4	Zacchaeus	Nr Heritage Centre	9
4	Blind Bartimaeus	Iona Community shop	10
4	Who is the greatest?	Road to Hostel	11
5	These stones shout	Columba's Bay	12
6	Last Supper	St Michael's Chapel	13
6	Mount of Olives	Abbey Garden	14
6	Trial of Jesus	Cloisters	15
6	Crucifixion	St Martin's Cross	16
6	Resurrection	Oran's Chapel	17
6	Emmaus Road	Road of the Dead	18
6	Ascension	Hill by Abbey	19

The number column refers to the map of Iona on the previous page.

On day one there is time to include a read-through of a written version of the gospel to help everyone orientate to the task and to provide a few memory joggers for the rest of the week. Any written gospel can be chosen. For the week described here we chose Luke but it could be done with Mark (as in the Lake District example given previously) or with Matthew or John if preferred. (The choice will be personal or may depend on the current lectionary year.) The subsequent RB pilgrimage can be compressed into a few days or spread out for longer if the time is available. Reading a whole gospel aloud like this will take approximately two hours. It's also fine to leave it out.

Mark time [13]

Waiting
at the lakeside:
waves lapping,
mists embracing.

Waiting
in the graveyard:
grass greening,
clock striking.

Waiting
on the mountain:
sheep bleating,
stones encircling.

Waiting
on the hillside:
rain falling,
women watching.

Waiting
in the graveyard:
tomb empty,
people silent.

Waiting
at the lakeside:
bread breaking,
story telling.

He'll be coming down the mountain [14]

Fasting alone in the desert,
Tell of the days that are past.
How for our sins He was tempted,
Yet was triumphant at last.
Tell of the years of His labour,
Tell of the sorrow He bore.
He was despised and afflicted,
Homeless, rejected and poor.

Fanny Crosby

Even though doing RB outside like this can be very helpful, we
cannot always get out and about, and climbing mountains might
well be beyond quite a few of us. This RB about Jesus and mountains
can be done indoors as well as out.

There are a lot of stories about mountains in the Bible. Begin by
seeing how many you can remember. Here are a few to get you
started:

Noah's Ark comes to rest on Mount Ararat
Moses gets the Ten Commandments up a mountain
Isaiah prophesies about the mountain of the Lord

What is it about mountains that made them so special to the people
of the Bible? Ask participants to think about this in small groups and
collect up their answers on a flip chart. They might include responses
like these:

'The natural world is awesome'
'Mountains suggest danger'
'A sense of isolation'
'They seem majestic and mysterious'

Split the participants into smaller informal groups and ask the
groups to 'remember a story about Jesus going up a mountain'. Give
them some time to work together and then ask them to retell their
stories to the other groups. See which stories they have chosen.

The following examples come from three groups doing this remembering the Bible activity together:

Group 1 remembered the story of the Transfiguration:

> *'Jesus went up a mountain with some disciples and they thought they saw Moses and Elijah with him there. The disciples didn't really know what to make of it so they said, "We'll make some altars for them," but Moses and Elijah disappeared. Then Jesus was changed so that he seemed to be shining bright. A voice said, "This is my Son."'*

Group 2 remembered Jesus going into the wilderness:

> *'Jesus was in the wilderness and he was taken up a high mountain. The devil said, "All this you can see from here, it could be yours." And Jesus replied: "Push off! No way!"'*

Group 3 began by remembering something else:

> *'This boy went up a mountain with his Dad because his Dad thought he should kill him for a sacrifice to God – though we're not really sure why. But he didn't have to kill him because there was a sheep there stuck in a bush. They caught that and used it instead.'*

This turned out to be the story of Abraham taking Isaac up a mountain. However, according to the principles of RB it was not wrong. Rather than respond with 'That's not the one we're doing today,' a further conversation developed. Having listened to what Group 1 had said, Group 3 said:

> *'Maybe Jesus had gone up the mountain to try to understand God's plan for him. Some bits of the plan were good and some bits were bad but at least now he was prepared for what would happen.'*

Following the remembering you might like to discuss some of the following:

- What happened when Jesus got down the mountain? (See *Word of Mouth*, pages 109-112.)
- In the Bible, mountains are often a place of change: why?
- What sort of places change us and why?

You might want to end with this version of a well known song ...

> *He'll be coming down the mountain when he comes.*
> *He'll be coming down the mountain when he comes.*
> *He'll be coming down the mountain, coming down the mountain,*
> *Coming down the mountain when he comes.*

Make up verses to reflect the remembering and discussions you have had rather than the 'He'll be wearing pink pyjamas' of the more usual version.

Creating winsome places for RB

When doing RB it helps if the place is attractive, welcoming and comfortable. Stale biscuits and weak orange squash should not be on the menu. Here are some ideas.

Food
Food is the most winsome of things for nearly everyone and it can help to make a place attractive, comfortable, welcoming and unthreatening. Getting food right is important. Have plenty of choices so that as many people as possible feel included. Not eating is also a reasonable option: don't force people to eat, and be alert to the silence people might have about food. When different faith groups meet together and eat, it is particularly important to plan the food beforehand and label it so people know what it is. Food can help to create an informal and even chaotic atmosphere which is more favourable to RB than stiff formality.

Food is particularly good in a situation where there are six people in a space made for four hundred and they all sit as far away from each other as possible. Try a tube of something. They will have to move closer together to pass it round. Providing food is a good way of showing that anyone can eat whilst worshipping, praying, remembering the Bible or whatever. If it is someone's birthday, have a cake. If it is a day for being wobbly, then have some jelly. If it is a day for thinking about justice, then have some scrummy fair trade items.

If you can fit the food to the remembering theme, so much the better. Fish and bread are obvious examples as they crop up in the gospels a few times. But there are also figs (cursed or otherwise), a fatted calf and other things that could be brought to life with a bit of creative thinking. Better still, actually make the stuff together and then eat it. This may need some 'here's some I began to make a bit earlier' ingenuity if time is limited.

> *Food-wise God, in our making and baking*
> *may we take time to examine ourselves.*

Help us to be honest and truthful
and attend to the details of our relationships.
As the dough grows
so may this be a time of growth for us.
As the smell of newly baked bread
creates an inviting atmosphere
so may we be made new.

Space

Dull places are not winsome. A place does not have to be lively to be
winsome but it does need life. A dead place is obvious. It has an air
about it and various signs of neglect. That does not mean everything
has to be new, but it does need to seem looked after, valued and cared
for. Light also helps. A low lighting budget may save on the elec-
tricity bill but it doesn't help those who need to see faces to
remember them or to hear better what is being said.

One of the things that can make space very appealing is to have
displays of what happens there. This involves photos or pictures of
different activities up on the walls or on display boards – not for ever,
but until the next winsome thing happens. A community education
group or toddler group who sees, the next time it meets, that its
work is part of a display in the church for everyone to reflect on has
a new sense of belonging in the space, which is much more welcoming than the old curtains or the peeling paint. Folk will gather
around a display and look to see 'Am I there?' or 'Look, there you
are!' It will be fun and it will be a chance to reflect on what was going
on. Even if you were not part of that activity, it gives everyone a
chance to see just what does happen in the everyday life of the winsome church. If you have a website, do the displays there but
remember to keep them up to date.

It requires imagination and time to keep the displays fresh, so it is
a good idea to identify some people who are good at it and who can
nurture others in the doing of it. Many things can be used for displays
and the displays themselves can be part of the RB too. I often ask
those whose work is in a display what bits of the Bible it reminds them

of, tapping into their remembered Bibles, and then I try to weave that and their reflections on the activity back into the sessions we have together. It is this continued weaving together of space, people, activities and RB that begins to offer the possibility of community.

God of space, outer, inner and virtual,
space us out with your presence
that we may connect with each other
and with the earth so making community
a place where all may live.

On the move with Jesus or moving on with Jesus

The aim of this activity is to explore the importance of itineracy in Jesus' ministry and its implications for our own lives.

How long does it take?
This kind of activity can take 20-30 minutes or several days or weeks depending on whether you want to just dip your toe into the idea or fully immerse yourself in it. It's the kind of thing you can decide to explore consistently over a period of time or just revisit now and again. It's something you can do literally, i.e. by moving about, or in your imagination, i.e. by thinking about moving around.

Approach to the Bible
Needless to say, I am using RB here. But that doesn't mean you can't use written Bibles or refer to them from time to time if you want to. Indeed, most of us probably use a combination of remembered and written Bibles on our faith journey. Equally, the scholarship that has informed this work has come from several different sources, so be eclectic. Most people discovering discipleship are just that.

To begin
One thing you might recall about Jesus' life and ministry was that he

was always on the move. He was always going somewhere or coming from somewhere else. He is depicted as a travelling teacher and healer who, although he had settled origins in a village in Galilee, spent a significant part of his adult life without a fixed address.

The place
It's a good idea to plan to do this somewhere real. The place might be local, the street on which you live, the local neighbourhood or community, or a place you frequently visit. Or it might be a new place or one rarely visited but chosen for its significance, either personal or communal. Whichever of these kinds of places you choose, we shall call this experience 'pilgrimage'. Now, that word has some particular connotations. It has been used for many generations to describe journeys associated with sacred ritual. Jesus himself seems to have taken part in this kind of journey at different times in his life. All I am doing is asking you to extend the notion to embrace not just your favourite holiday or retreat destination but any journey on which you engage in faith-filled contemplation of Jesus and his life and ministry. In other words, you could do it on the bus tomorrow, or when you next go to Jerusalem. By all means plan in advance when and where you want to do this – but, equally, doing it fairly spontaneously at any time is also valuable.

The atmosphere
It's important to take in the atmosphere of the place and the whole feel of the journey. You can do this from memory. But if you do it live, think about how it feels. What information are your senses conveying to you about what is happening as you take the journey you are on? Pose yourself questions like:

- What feels good?
- What feels uncomfortable?
- What are my senses communicating to me about this place?

The Bible

Once you have centred yourself in the place and got a sense of how you feel about being there, begin to consider your RB and think about the journeys of Jesus. Think about one particular journey you remember. Where was it to? Where was it from? Who was there? What was happening? Try to reconstruct the itinerary of Jesus' journey as you are going on yours (you may want to stop a while to do this).

Retell the story to yourself. How does it feel to be on this journey with Jesus now? The journey you are making does not have to be a similar journey to the one you are remembering Jesus made. What is important is the experience of moving about, being itinerant. Some of us have choices about when and where we go, and some do not. Choosing to reflect on Jesus' journeying whilst ourselves making a journey may help us to connect afresh with the itinerant nature of discipleship.

If using a written Bible, read the passage you have chosen and ask yourself the questions above.

Moving on

As your physical (or remembered) journey progresses there may be times and places when you think of another Jesus journey and you spend a moment remembering that. It would be good to collect up a whole series of remembered Jesus journeys and the thoughts you have about them. This could all happen in one day, or one week or one month, or at least one lifetime. You might want to help your remembering by taking photos that remind you of the journeys, doing sketches or collecting stuff that reminds you of the places, and even writing a few notes to remind you which journey, when, where and what you thought about. Your journey journal will help you to keep track of your moves and thoughts during this time. It will be like a companion to your journey. You will build it up and refer back to it now and then.

Journaling about journeys

Here are some examples of journaling about journeys.

September, somewhere in the middle of England
It was a surprise to find it just like he said it would be, although the harvest has already been gathered. Wheat this year I think and potatoes last: a few tell-tale plants had resiliently pushed up between the rows.

The footpath that I was on made its diagonal way across the field and was baked every bit as hard as he'd said. A few old husks ground under other feet were all that was left on the path. A flock of voracious pigeons flew ahead of me, scattering as I approached. At least there was enough to see them through the days ahead.

I came to a group of stones at the corner of the field and a broken gate or stile. There was, as he predicted, nothing much growing there. Along the field boundaries brambles provided a feast for a few small creatures whilst thistles and nettles thronged viciously at their base. There was no place for crops here either.

So how can the poor survive, competing with pigeons and field mice for the pitifully small leftovers? Each year it seems we must learn the lesson again. Only if we are ready to share the harvest justly will we all live on.

Waiting at the door
I saw a single figure waiting at the door of a small church in the Flow Country in north Caithness. By the way he was dressed, clearly he was the minister. It was already after 3pm and only two cars were in the car park (his and the organist's?) as I pulled up to take a photograph. He waved and I returned the greeting. Who was the door open for? For whom was he waiting? I'd not been to church for weeks as we were on our way from Land's End to John O'Groats[15] with Bob. I had not missed it, largely because for forty years or so now the journey has continued in different ways. Even so, I cannot say what is round the next bend in the road.

Donkey-ology or travelling with a donkey
These days donkeys count for little. Their comical ears and slow gait make them unsuitable for celebrity transport and they are not fast enough for business class. As Mélanie Delloye says in her book about travels with a donkey, 'You cannot lock up a donkey and leave it alone in a parking place in the middle of town.'[16] Her donkey journey from Belgium to Portugal lasted from April 2003 to July 2006 and she was accompanied not just by donkeys but by her husband and two children as well. Several other people joined in different parts of the journey for a few days or so. Along the way there were plenty of opportunities for RB, although this was not the main purpose of her journey – more a spin off, if you like. Primarily she was interested in experiencing life in the slow lane: 'Even after several months of travelling with a donkey you have not got very far.'[17] Having chosen to go with a donkey, Delloye explains her thinking: 'Dogs guard, horses are imposing but donkeys let anyone come near.'[18]

There are three interesting pieces of RB in her book. First she remembers that Job had, amongst other things, a thousand female donkeys (we call them 'jennies' in English) before he found his fortunes changed. Donkeys are important aspects of wealth in some cultures.

Secondly, 'Donkeys are patient, give service and are not proud.'[19] She compares this to Paul's letter to the church at Corinth and his words about love: always patient and kind and not keeping a score of wrongs. Not being much of a Pauline scholar I don't tend to do RB with the letters of the New Testament. But I'm sure it's possible, with or without a donkey.

Thirdly of course there's RB on donkeys in the life of Jesus, from the flight into Egypt to Palm Sunday. How many more silent, unnamed donkeys were witnesses to his life and ministry? Maybe you'd like to take a journey with a donkey and think about this. In her last paragraph she muses about what to call this life with donkeys, the travels and reflections that it enabled. Her term for it is 'L'ânalogie' (from the French *âne*, donkey) which I translate as 'donkey-ology'. Give it a try.

Cross-marked beast
bearing the cross-burdened one,
what do you say now
or bray somehow?
Stumbling on a stony track,
people's coats on your back,
a shouting crowd in your ear:
how does it now appear?
Doing your job you might say
carrying him homewards today;
yesterday's weight forgotten,
tomorrow's burden still uncertain.

Prayers about journeys ...

The long road[20]

Christ of the long road,
you called us to discipleship
and call us again to renewed commitment.
Help us to sort out our priorities,
and deal with our disappointments.
Sustain us on the road that leads
from baptism to your just kingdom.
With your word alive in us,
give us life to live, life to share
and life to celebrate.

Still travelling[21]

Where the roar of the jet
and the glow of the afterburner
had gone
the geese came next,
calling loudly,
travelling together,
always changing shape.

Wild Spirit,
do not let us be tamed
to a life made only
of straight lines.
May we also travel
like the geese,
sharing the load
enjoying the lift,
calling encouragement:
just flying.

Fish for people[22]

'Fish for people' is what he told us. But nowadays there's not much fish for people here. You can see what it used to be like and there are still a few people around to tell the story, but today we don't do much fishing for people or anyone else.

It was always a hard life. The sea is unpredictable and dangerous in all parts of the world. Beautiful too in its own way, but savage and raw. We all knew this. All of us had families that were marked by it. A father, husband or son taken; a wife, mother or siblings left. Then there were those that survived with terrible memories and scars.

'Fish for people,' he said and we looked at him like 'What would he know?' – a carpenter and from Nazareth! But he was persistent, compelling and we tried it again and got more than we bargained for. So that fired us up and off we went, some of us. Others remained to feed families and communities left behind. We'd come back from time to time, when the season dictated. We were not lovers of the land. For all its perilous cruelty we preferred the sea.

Afterwards, looking back, it was obvious we would return here, but things had changed in us and around us. We'd seen and heard things that lodged inside us and made itchy memories. Some left for a second time, compelled by a vision missed by others. Some stayed, anchored by family and community ties, but none of us were ever the same again.

We told the stories of the Fishing One, the one who thought of people like fish and who wanted us to go after them and haul them into the kingdom he spoke about. The tales were passed on as the fish came and went. Times changed and fisher-folk changed too. There's not so much fishing today, not so many fish: empty harbours, upturned boats, the tide still comes and goes.

If you look over to the other shore now, you can still imagine him walking by, urging us to fish for people. But we are old and tired and marooned by time and tide. We no longer think we can fish for people. We'd like him to come back, reassure us, fire us up again, but we are afraid it is too late. It's a long time since we saw anyone walk on water.

To use this story
Try to tell it in your own words rather than read it word for word. It goes well on a beach in the early morning with the smell of barbecued fish wafting under your nostrils. Get a fair trade portable barbecue and either catch your own fish or buy it from someone who has caught some (line fishing is one sustainable way of fishing). Make sure you clear up after your beach breakfast.

Notes

[13] From a week remembering the Bible in the Lake District, June 2005.
[14] Based on Remembering the Bible at Shiregreen United Reformed Church on 04.03.2007.
[15] Bob did this on foot in 2003.

[16] From Delloye (2009), page 26. Note that the book is in French and this is my informal oral translation (i.e. I have not made a formal written translation of this document).

[17] ibid. page 21.

[18] ibid. page 26.

[19] ibid. page 38.

[20] For Shrewsbury URC 2009.

[21] Overlooking RAF Lossiemouth, February 2007.

[22] For the Thames North and Eastern Synod Ministers' Spring School, Lindisfarne, April 2009.

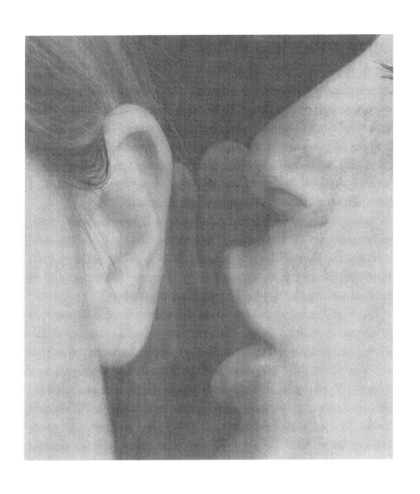

Chapter five

Remembering what

Remembering what

There are many challenges to using the remembered Bible process in our contemporary situation.[23] In Western Europe we do not now live in the predominantly oral culture of first-century Palestine. Even if there are remnants of this culture here and there, from newcomers and artists of different kinds, disabled people and other edge-dwellers, the mainstream of our culture is now highly literate, and this is also true of the mainstream of the church.

Furthermore, some biblical scholars would have difficulty with the remembered Bible process. The written Bible still has ultimate authority for many. The remembered Bible is rather hit and miss. What sticks in our memories and why? If we use this version all of the time, will we just use the bits we like or agree with?

These and other questions about the remembered Bible process are important to think about. I believe they point to a number of different considerations. Firstly, ordinary people do want to engage with the Bible. Not everyone will be able to use highly literate methods. Working inclusively with people of all ages and abilities will require appropriate tools, of which remembering the Bible could be one. Secondly, remembering the Bible does not preclude other methods being used. Often folk who have taken part in remembering activities will go on to listen to or read for themselves from the written Bible.

Some of the gains from using the remembered Bible process include:

- the energy released, the sound generated;
- the listening and sharing that take place;
- hearing local ordinary voices for a change;
- the collaboration of people helping each other to remember;
- the creation of a safe place for faith to be explored.

As the buzz gets going around the remembering tasks and the different remembered bits are brought together, energy can be released for social transformation. The space, once silent or only occupied by specific voices, is now shared by ordinary people. Finding a voice is an essential part of growing self-confidence and self-esteem. These are crucial first steps on the path to social transformation. Collaboration is an essential skill in community-building. It requires practice. This can all happen when we remember the Bible together.

If there is a concern that some voices are being missed, or some bits of the Bible are being overlooked, then it is always possible to invite someone to bring this voice or insight into the remembering process.

Finally, it is important to say that this process is not just for noisy, confident extroverts, either as participants or facilitators. There are many ways of remembering the Bible. These can be loud and wacky or quietly meditative. If it doesn't work for you the first time, then try it again, perhaps in another space or place or in a different way. Most of all, if you try it, keep track of how it goes. Write your own stories and reflections, and make pictures and images, dances and drama around the process as a way of recording what is happening. This will all help you to see where to go next when remembering the Bible together.

Lazarus, come out!

I don't know what got you in there.
I can't say for sure that you and your family
share the same story as these numerous others,
added to daily by accident, carelessness, deliberate action, war or ...

All I know is that some said you were the silent one.
silent before death: unheard in the home you shared.
Unremarkable, ordinary guy.
Silent as death: four days in the tomb,
stinking, abandoned guy.
Silent after death, called out with weeping,
bound and gagged, barely blinking guy.

All I know is that he said it:
Release him!
Get him out of there!
Give him another chance!
Make it possible for him to live again!

All I know is that he,
the weeping one,
the calling one,
the agonised one,
waited there
until you were free.

And then
downhill to Jerusalem,
and a date with history
that shattered the ordinary
and made us all extraordinary for ever.

Now it's your turn.
Lazarus, come out!

How to use this poem
You could use this poem at the end of an RB session on the story of
Lazarus or a series of stories in Lent or Holy Week.

Cana wedding

Chorus
> *Tell the story, sing the song,*
> *Dance for joy and come along,*
> *This is where we all belong:*
> *That party, Cana's wedding!*

1. Wine it seems had all run out:
   'Ask my son,' she had no doubt,
   'He will help you sort it out,'
   At that Cana wedding.

2. Servants got the jars and filled
   Each with water as he willed;
   Not a drop of it was spilled,
   At that Cana wedding.

3. Everyone was quite surprised,
   Turned to wine before their eyes:
   'Kept the best till last – how wise!'
   At that Cana wedding.

Tune: Mairi's Wedding

How to use this song
You could use this song in an RB session, either as a concluding piece or as a bit of a break in the middle. Jesus at the wedding at Cana is something often remembered by groups and the tune, which is fast and furious, makes this song popular. It is good on a violin or with a group of ceilidh musicians.

Playing with more parables

The parables of Jesus were an oral community education curriculum. This curriculum had two main branches: social and political understanding and peacemaking. It is Herzog who puts forward the view that Jesus was trying to educate ordinary people about the social and political structures of his time, whilst Beavis advances the opinion that the parables were a force for social cohesion and reconciliation (Herzog, 1994; Beavis, 2002). In this section we shall examine the layers of silence that are woven into the parables and propose some alternative readings and renditions.

It's important when discussing Herzog's methods to understand the structure of first-century Palestinian society. Here's a way of doing that which involves the Nativity Play dressing-up box (the old curtains, tea towels, etc).

According to Herzog, first-century Palestine was a bottom-heavy society with the top position being held by the king – a despot and not at all nice. Have someone dress up as the king. Beneath the king were the royal family and court officials. Have a few people dress up as these. Whilst they did what the king wanted they were in favour. If not they were out. There was a small merchant class and a small retainer class. In the first group were those who bought and sold stuff, not always fair trade, and in the latter, scribes, priests and civil servants who could read and write and keep the wheels of state turning, again not always fairly. Have a few people dress up like this. The majority of people were peasants, a few of whom were also artisans, like carpenters. This group ranged from those who could get by economically most of the time to those who hardly ever did (subsistence farmers). Few of them owned much and it is particularly important to remember that most did not own the land they worked. The land was owned by landowners in the higher classes. Peasants paid taxes to work it and the tax system was rarely fair. Because this was the majority of the population, don't have anyone dress up as these: just tell most of the rest of the group that this is their role. Beneath the peasants were the underclass, the unclean and degraded who for one reason or another were falling, or had fallen, out of society. These reasons included illness, like leprosy, and disability, debt and criminality. Have a few people be degraded and unclean, as this is an important group when it comes to parables.

When explaining the structure of first-century Palestinian society, invite each group to identify themselves in turn. If there's time, encourage them to talk to each other and other groups to think about what life would have been like.

If dressing up is not the kind of thing that comes naturally or the dressing-up box has already been booked by another group of people, try to have a diagram of the social situation (see next page) either on a PowerPoint, on an overhead projector or in a handout for people to look at.

When remembering the parables together, it is important to identify what part of society Jesus is telling his story about. Is it about upper or middle class people who own land and have servants or slaves in their households? Is it about peasants and peasant life: widows who lose coins and their entire economic security, for example? Is it about the most marginalised or dispossessed of people, the excluded ones who have next to nothing so they have to rob to live (as in the story of the Good Samaritan)? Is it about the religious, social or economic divisions of the day: the Samaritan versus the priest and the Levite, for example? Most of all, what are we to understand about society and how to build better community as a result of the story? Try to get to the heart of this rather than just say, 'I've heard it before.'

A simplified diagram to represent the relationship between classes in 1st-century Palestine (after Herzog 2005)

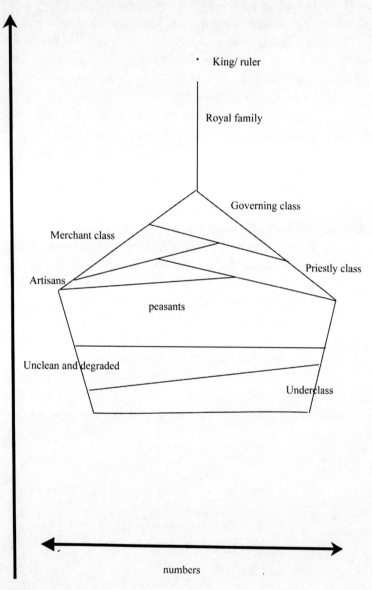

The Parable of the Unforgiven Servant [24]

It's a 'dog-eat-dog world' says Herzog of the Parable of the Unforgiven Servant. We can think of many 'dog-eat-dog' examples in our own world that might be useful starting points for reflecting on this parable. We also need to understand the world of the court retainer in first-century Palestine.

So we need a modern parable for the former and a sketch for the latter, which could be based on the well known 'class sketch' by John Cleese, Ronnie Barker and Ronnie Corbett from *The Frost Report*.

Retainers sketch
Take three people – one tall, one of medium height and one short. Stand them in height order. Give them notices to hold. The tallest holds a notice that says 'King' on one side and 'Ruler' on the other. The second holds a notice that says 'Servant' on one side and 'I can read' on the other. The third holds a notice that says 'Other servant' on one side and 'I can't read' on the other. They hold the notices with the first side showing. The third person could hold theirs upside down. The dialogue is as follows:

1.	I look down on them because I am the king.
2 & 3.	We look up to him because he is the king.
1.	They do what I say because I am the king.
2.	I do what he says because he is the king and he *[indicates 3]* does what I say because I am the important servant.
3.	I know my place.
2.	Although he looks down on me because he is the king, he needs me because I am an important servant. He also needs me because I am a more important servant than him *[indicates 3]*.
3.	I know my place.
	[turn cards over]
1.	The king is the ruler. The king is in charge. What the king says everyone obeys. There is only one king.

2 & 3.	There are lots of servants. We know our place.
2.	I know my place. I can read so it is my place to be a scribe or a functionary, or a dealer for the ruler. I have an important position. The king's wealth is in my hands.
3. *(to 2)*	What does this say? *[pointing to notice]*
2.	Can't you read?
3.	No, I can't read. I am only good for menial tasks like manual labour and torture. I know my place.
1. *(to 2)*	You owe me money, a lot of money. Pay up or else be sold as a slave.
2.	Mercy, O kind King! I cannot pay. Do not sell me and my family into slavery. Mercy, mercy! I will do better next time.
1.	I forgive your debts. Make sure you do better next time.
2.	Thank you, O kind King. *(To 3)* Oi you. You owe me money. Not as much as I owed him, but you owe me just the same. Hand it over or get lost, very lost.
3.	I cannot pay, have mercy!
2.	Not a chance.
1.	What is this I hear? Was I not merciful to you? Yet I hear you have not been merciful to him *[indicates 3]*. You horrible servant. You shall be thrown into prison and tortured. Where is the torturer?
3.	I am the torturer.

How to use this sketch

This sketch is a good way of demonstrating the relationships between the characters in this parable and revealing the power at work in the first-century context.

The Parable of the Gardener and the Potting Sheds[25]

There was a gardener who was invited to garden in a new landscape. This landscape was very varied, made up as it was of places from wild countryside to urban wastelands. Dotted around the landscape were a number of potting sheds. Some of the potting sheds were small and some were larger, some were new and some were older, some were in good repair and some needed significant attention. Each potting shed had its own local gardeners: old and young, experienced and novices. Some sheds had a few and some had a few more. The new gardener wondered what to do in the landscape.

The gardener began by visiting the potting sheds, the wild countryside and the urban wastelands. In each place the gardener noted what was thriving and what was struggling. The gardener met many other gardeners and noted how they did their gardening: some formed committees and talked a lot about gardening; like *Gardeners' Question Time* some asked the new gardener lots of questions; some looked things up in gardening books; some wanted to spruce up their potting shed and open it up to other gardeners; some wanted to keep the potting shed to themselves; some liked to get their hands dirty and side by side with the new gardener to transplant seedlings and take cuttings.

The new gardener liked to take some of the seedlings and cuttings along whilst travelling through the landscape and share them with other gardeners, both those in potting sheds and those in the wild countryside and the urban wastelands. The new gardener also liked to encourage the other gardeners to try new plants, to experiment with the soil and conditions and the other activities of the potting shed: plant sales, barbecues, making jam and the like. Sometimes there were difficult situations to face: a decision to move a plant out of the potting shed, thinking that the frosts were over for the winter, might backfire and a sudden late frost take all the gardeners by surprise. There was global warming and increased flood risk to face in some places, and unsafe or unused potting sheds in others.

The new gardener didn't have the answers to all these questions, only a deep and passionate commitment to gardening. The new gardener knew that gardening is unpredictable at times, that it calls for time, patience and respect. Gardeners need an ability to cope with setbacks and a sure and solid hope that the sun will rise every day. Each day the new gardener would give thanks for this and go out to meet the other gardeners and garden with them, confident that we are all still growing.

How to use this story
This story is written as an allegory, which is a common form of parable. It could serve as an example of that sort of parable on the theme of mission or leadership. Tell the story in your own words if you can, rather than read it out.

Bible kennings

What are kennings?
Kennings are Anglo-Saxon word pairs. The pattern is easy to pick up, consisting of a noun (or adjective) and a verb. Kennings provide a fun way of summarising the most memorable aspects of a story and so enhance our remembering. Here's an example by Hannah for the Parable of the Lost Sheep. It has two stanzas: one about the sheep and one about the shepherd.

Grass eater
Jumper crafter
Money maker
Fold leaver
Bleat producer
Shepherd lover

Flock guarder
Meat herder

Wool keeper
Feed provider
Animal searcher
Sheep finder [26]

How to do group Bible kennings [27]

After a remembered version (or a narrated or read version if necessary) ask people for a 'word storm' on the story – any words they can think of at all about the story. Put them all down on a large flip chart. Then begin to arrange them in pairs – some contributors may do this more readily than others, but people often get the hang of it as it goes along. One or more people might then arrange the word pairs to tell the story again as in this example on the Parable of the Good Samaritan:

Good Samaritan kennings [28]

Journey maker
Lonely-road trotter

   Cowardly attacker
   Body breaker
   Money taker

     Death defier

      Victim ignorer
      Other-side walker

        Donkey leader
        Wound binder
        Money giver
        Need provider

NOTES

[23] This reflection is based on responses to the paper 'Remember that?' which I gave at the Community Work Exposed event at Shiregreen United Reformed Church on 5th March 2007. Thanks to John Campbell for initiating the response.

[24] Matthew 18:21-35

[25] For the Yorkshire Synod of the United Reformed Church.

[26] By Hannah Warwicker, used with permission. First appeared in 'A New Heaven and a New Earth', URC Prayer Handbook 2006/7

[27] More about doing kennings like this can be found at http://www.vision4life.org.uk/index.php/bible-year/desserts/kennings-and-cookies/

[28] Hannah Warwicker and Members of Trinity URC Sheffield, November 2006.

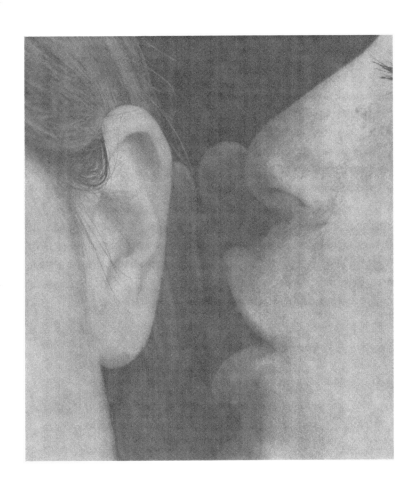

Chapter six

Remembering One

Remembering One

Ultimately we come to the heart of the remembered gospel – the
One whom we are remembering. Without him there would be no
point, no centre, no life. In this section we concentrate on teasing
out who Jesus is to us and what that means for our communities. It
is important, when reflecting on who Jesus is for us, to allow plenty
of time for listening. In a decade that has seen many polarised
debates regarding Jesus, whether about his humanity versus his
divinity, his socio-economic status as a refugee, his social class as an
artisan, or his sexuality, plenty of different views about Jesus have
emerged. It is important to accord each participant the respectful
space in which they can build up their own confidence to answer
Jesus' question: 'Who am I?'

Who am I? A game

What is it?
It's a card game about Jesus that can vary in length depending on the
time available, the setting and the number of people taking part.

Aim
To explore who Jesus is, using things we remember about him so that
we can listen to each other and share our insights.

Remembering Jesus
We all remember different things about Jesus. This may be a huge
generalisation, but if we all have a Bible in us, it will include things
we have remembered about Jesus. As we try to follow him ourselves,
it is these remembered things that inform our actions on a daily
basis. So just what do we remember about Jesus and, as a result of
this remembering, who do we say he is?

You will need
Some small cards or pieces of paper with a description of Jesus written on each using the kennings pattern described in the previous section: for example Donkey rider, Bread sharer. A list of possible descriptions, to which you can add your own, is given later in this section.

You might want enough cards for one per table if you are doing this in a lunch club; enough for one for each person if you are doing it in the Elders' meeting; enough for one between two if you are doing it at the church meeting; or enough for one between 4-6 people if you are doing it in small groups; or one between two for an activity in pairs.

This activity can be done with people of all ages and abilities. If your group includes people who communicate without speech then the whole activity can be done non-verbally with drama, mime, symbols or pictures, for example by drawing or acting out the kennings on the card.

Some ground rules
When remembering the Bible together, remind people this is not a test. Different people will remember different things. This is not a game for clever people to show off to others but for all of us to listen and build up shared understandings. Remind people not to interrupt each other. Also, ask them not to judge the stories told by others. It is particularly unhelpful to use the terms 'right' or 'wrong' to describe people's remembered stories. Each person should be encouraged to own their own version of the story they remember.

To begin
Tell the group that we are going to see what we remember about Jesus. Give out the small cards, depending on the size of the group and how long you intend to run the activity. Invite people to consider the words on their card and see what story about Jesus they remember that links to these words. If they are working in pairs or small groups, give them some time to tell each other these stories. If they are working as individuals, give them time to think about the

story and how they will tell it.

Note that you can run this activity more than once by varying the cards you give out or the number of people considering each card. To begin with, try to choose descriptions of Jesus that link to well known stories that seem to be at the heart of the remembered Bible – and let people do the task with others rather than alone. On the whole, it's best not to put people on the spot. Speaking for yourself can be scary until you feel confident enough.

Whilst people are remembering, try to listen to what you hear coming from the groups, as you may want to refer to some of these ideas later.

Depending on the time available, invite one or more groups to tell what they have remembered. Ask other participants to listen to these rememberings and not interrupt.

Prayer
End the activity with prayer:

> *Companion Christ,*
> *You are to us as …*
> [insert some of the words used by the group here]
> *Come alive in our lives*
> *as we listen and share our stories with others.*
> *Amen*

For the cards
Here are some descriptions of Jesus to put on the cards, to which you can add your own.

Mother amazer
Father confuser
Shepherd surpriser
King confounder
Temple visitor
Obedient developer
Desert dweller
Disciple caller
Roof raiser
Crowd gatherer
Home comer
Story teller
Fishermen finder
Hillside teacher
Enemy lover
Prayer instructor
Eye examiner
Sparrow sparer
Hair counter
Seed sower
Water walker
Storm calmer
People feeder
Child blesser
Leper healer
Hillside pray-er
Rule breaker
Mind changer
Faith affirmer
Mountain climber

Sin forgiver
Spirit challenger
Baptism sharer
Road traveller
Water drinker
Back straightener
Tear shedder
Temple talker
Widow encourager
Donkey rider
Tree curser
Table turner
Commandment endorser
Foot washer
Supper sharer
Bread breaker
Garden pray-er
Crown wearer
Pain bearer
Cross carrier
Torture forgiver
Death confronter
Stone mover
Dawn gardener
Name caller
Tomb quitter
Onward traveller
Wound bearer
Power promiser
Footprint leaver

Who do you say that I am?

We each tell stories in different ways. If we told our own stories of Jesus, each one would be different. Yet people do sometimes ask me how to tell a story, or at least how to get started, particularly in ways that open up people's memories rather than closing them down. Whilst it is difficult to be prescriptive about this, the following paragraphs may act as a story-starter or memory-jogger to go alongside the kennings of Jesus given in the previous section. They are based around some of the stories of Jesus that seem, from my work over the last decade and a half, to be amongst the most remembered. The concluding poems or prayers may be used at the end of an RB session or may help you to generate your own ideas to use in worship sessions of different sorts. Once you get the gist of it you will think of others. The more you practise, the more confidence you will gain in telling your own story of Jesus. One story will quite probably link into other stories because that is how memory works.

One thing you may notice is the presence of layers of meaning and some ambiguity both in what is written here and in what folks remember together. Oral versions of the gospel exist in more versions and have more ambiguity than the few written versions of the printed Bible. They also often contain additional examples of 'play on words' because oral language often uses that to help retain memories. As these notes and prayer poems are the result of real RB sessions, they also bear these marks.

1   Mother amazer

Right from the beginning of the story of his life, we meet Jesus as one who amazed people, even his own mother. You might say that most women are justifiably amazed by pregnancy but the story that we have of Mary's pregnancy is a mix of ordinary and extraordinary experiences that add up to one of the most memorable pregnancies in history. After its announcement by an angel, Mary is soon singing a first rate song of rebellion and subversion. After that a trip to visit relatives seems an anticlimax until the presence of the baby in Mary's womb has the other (the future John the Baptist) dancing in his own mother's womb. Not one amazed mother, but two.

You may be able to think of other stories in which Jesus amazed his own mother, or other mothers. You may also make links to other stories about his mother. For example, it is in the third verse of the carol 'God rest you merry gentlemen' that Mary is described as 'a virgin bright':

Mary was bright

Mary was bright:
even the most merry gentlemen said so.
She was bright enough
to know her forebears
and look out for the patterns of God's doing.
She was bright enough
to want the world to change:
poor on top,
rich at the bottom.
She was bright enough to say 'Yes' to God
and mean it.

2 Father confuser

Jesus also confused people, even his own father. You might say any father could be surprised, even confused, after news of an unexpected pregnancy, but once again this pregnancy has extraordinary effects on others, adding to the layers of memory wrapped around this story. After another angel, and a vivid dream, Joseph finds himself agreeing to marry Mary to become the surrogate father of a child not his own, a decision that would set him on a number of different journeys, including the final one into relative obscurity. We know little enough about Joseph, but we do know he was confused, a common enough feeling and starting point.

Remembering Joseph can be challenging, but often he is linked with woodworking through his remembered profession as a carpenter. Remembering the role wood plays in the gospel story can be a way of linking Joseph and Jesus.

Through the wood

God, you call us through the wood;
through the wood you speak to us.
May we, your wood-wise ones,
touch wood with you,
hang on to your promises
and help shape the dreams of community
that only cross-wise commitment brings.

3 Shepherd surpriser

The surprises continued once the new family found their way to Bethlehem. At first unable to find a place to stay, they were welcomed into a stable and Mary gave birth there. The local working people – some shepherds spending the night on the hillside as usual – were surprised by more angels, music, singing and strange prophecies. Even so, they responded to this strange introduction and went to visit the family, later telling everyone they met about the experience. It was the kind of thing you might expect to stay with you all your life, like seeing a UFO or some other unexplainable event. If it happened to you, what would you say?

There are many biblical stories about shepherds, including quite a few outside the gospels. This common, low-status occupation was one Jesus himself often drew on for images and examples in his storytelling. Think of low-status occupations from our own culture, like cleaners, to find a possible link in modern urban society, although in a rural setting agricultural work continues to be low paid and low status.

Sheep aspirations

To play with wolves and whatnot is our aspiration.
To be out there in the great outdoors,
hefting* on a steep, rough fell in all weathers,
or so we think.
But how many of us are really up for it?
Isn't the timidity of our species,
the herd instinct and our preference for the familiar
what keeps us in here?

* Hefting – a term applied to breeds of hill sheep like Herdwick which find their way around the fells by a territorial instinct passed from one generation to another.

4 King confounder

Jesus' early influence extended beyond his family and immediate community. It went as far as the royal palace before he was even out of swaddling clothes. Others were waiting for news of a significant birth – how many we're not sure, but they were wealthy and wise. Having seen a star they followed it and ended up in the royal palace asking a despotic, insecure ruler questions that made him believe his throne was threatened. No wonder he was worried. He tried to have the wise ones and the baby traced, and when that failed used genocide to secure his own power. It could have happened yesterday: unmarked graves, the disappeared, cruelty and the abuse of power. And all this over a baby. So what sort of baby would that be then?

There are other stories that link Jesus to this royal family: his time as a refugee in Egypt, for example, and the massacre of the innocents – the babies of Bethlehem that were left behind.

Innocent enough

How can we look forward to the massacre of the innocents? [29]
Or get ready to hear Rachel weep again?
I'm not a media mogul getting rich on world exclusives,
or a weary newsreader on a 24-hour shift to spread the word,
but I have seen these scenes before:
mothers cradling their dead children,
their faces torn apart by tragedy and grief,
and I need to know they are remembered
by God and all humanity.
As Mary and Joseph carried Jesus to safety in Egypt
may we carry him in our lives
mindful of his innocent way of connecting us to each other.

5 Temple visitor

There are few written-down stories of Jesus' childhood, yet he must have had one. Of the few incidents recorded, the visit to the temple when he was on the verge of puberty is interesting for its implied early teenage rebellion. I find it is one of the most often remembered stories in RB sessions. Jesus decides to stay on in Jerusalem rather than return home with the rest of the community. His family do not realise and then become frantic when they fail to locate him in the larger group. Meanwhile, back in the temple Jesus is trying to do what so many young people have attempted: to get the religious powers-that-be to listen to the views of a young person. He seems to have had some success. They are astonished at what he knows. Listen hard enough and you can still hear that voice in young people the world over.

Teenage temple geek

You argued,
you had your say,
stated your case and kept them listening.
Your parents just didn't get it.
As for the neighbours,
were they ever going to?
But where would you be?
What would you be doing?
Anyone who could see that might get a life.

6 Obedient developer

But the rebellion was over for the time being. Perhaps the time was
not yet right. Whatever the reason Jesus went back home with his
family and nothing more is recorded for several years. Only his obe-
dience is remarked on. The early influences on our beliefs and values
are factors that shape our future development. As we read between
the lines of what little we know about the early influences on Jesus'
life, we get a glimpse of a strong sense of purpose from an early age.
His life in family and community must have provided him with suf-
ficient personal resources for the choices he made as an adult.

Life is rough

Notice on a church door in Huddersfield:
'UK Abrasives, please use side door'

'Life is rough,' said my friend,
when I pointed out the notice.
And I thought it's no accident
Jesus was a carpenter:
smoothing rough edges,
making the crooked straight,
tapering joints for a better fit.
There's a lot to it
when you're preparing a mission,
gearing up to be the Life Giver.
And I often wonder
how frequently he shuddered
when someone casually said,
'Pass the nails.'

Companion Christ,
with us in the rough and smooth,
may the life we share with you
be marked out on us

so that none can mistake whose we are
and who we follow.

7 Baptism sharer

The story of Jesus' baptism is a good one for remembering, particularly when baptising others or renewing baptismal vows. Sharing a
common baptism is another point of contact between us and Jesus.
John the Baptist, or the Baptiser as some call him, is a good character
for remembering, with his distinctive clothing and diet. I have a tin
of fried grasshoppers that my mother won in a raffle when I was
eight years old. These always come in handy for remembering John
the Baptist and his insect-based diet.

Baptism transformed Jesus and it transforms us. Acknowledged
as God's beloved and the one in whom God delights, Jesus is also
ready to share this special relationship with us too: we are beloved
and God delights in us.

> Living wet
>
> May we, like Jesus,
> live wet:
> wet from the waters of chaos
> breaking over the earth;
> wet from the waters of baptism
> breaking over our bodies;
> wet from the living water
> breaking over our lives.
> Bless us in earth, air and fire
> but most of all
> bless us in water;
> that anointed by the Life Giver
> we may follow the way.

8 Desert dweller

Those who visit the desert may be astonished by its beauty but none can overlook the harsh nature of the environment. It is both physically and emotionally demanding. Jesus stayed in the desert for forty days and nights, experiencing hunger and hallucinations. Stones could be bread. Each awesome vista felt like the top of the world, a place to rule from. Strange dreams and mirages contributed to a sense of testing and temptation. But he came through. There's no talk of what he took with him except a commitment to prayer and a balanced sense of self. In touch with God and with himself he was ready to be touched by the environment and come through to take up an even more gruelling journey.

> Lent in Iraq[30]
>
> Christ, in this desert
> accompany us
> on today's convoy
> and tomorrow's patrol,
> whether we swear or pray
> in your name.

9 Disciple caller

That journey would not be undertaken alone. His decision to invite companions leaves a lasting mark on them and him. Tradition concentrates on the men, but the group of people around him included women, and possibly whole families, at least from time to time. They came from diverse backgrounds representing the ordinary people of the era. That they decided to follow him says as much about them as him. Clearly he was compelling but they were ready to be compelled – ready to leave what they were used to and embrace all the uncertainty and hardship that might follow, which suggests it couldn't have looked any worse than the uncertainty and hardship they already faced. The story that unfolds is as much theirs as his, and by being theirs can become ours, the ordinary people of today.

When you consider doing RB around the theme of discipleship try not to confine yourself to only the obvious suspects. There were many who were called and many who still are.

Still calling

In joy and sorrow,
in gain and loss,
in despair and hope,
in death and life,
the Constant One,
calls me still.

10 Roof raiser

In the local towns and villages, houses were simple constructions and mostly flat-roofed. A large crowd might mean the front door was blocked but a resourceful group of friends could still get a sick person to meet Jesus by taking the roof off. If this surprised some of the locals, Jesus took it in his stride. Making eye contact with the man on the mat who has just appeared through a hole in the roof, Jesus assures him that he is forgiven. It is this statement that really takes the roof off for the crowd. Who is Jesus that he can forgive people? This is a role reserved in that society for a religious elite and accompanied by certain rituals. By taking the roof off this practice, Jesus is opening up the business of forgiveness to everyone and anyone who is looking for a new start.

Roof raiser

Roof raiser,
because you were there they took the roof off.
What would it take now to raise the roof?
What would it take to say, 'Your sins are forgiven?'

11   Crowd gatherer

Jesus' ministry in Galilee is marked by many large crowds. In the absence of large stadiums, major sporting events, or pop concerts and festivals, Jesus was like a travelling circus and roadshow. As a teacher and healer he attracted large crowds of people, many desperate for a new opportunity in life. Each crowd would have included a great diversity of people of various ages, nationalities, backgrounds, with different languages and expectations. All of them thronged to Jesus for their different reasons: curiosity has many forms.

> ### Meeting people
>
> You can meet the God of all creation
> in a supermarket or a factory.
> You can travel with the common Christ
> to a meadow or a high street.
> You can feel the fill of the Spirit
> on a mountaintop or in a waiting room.
> God has no second class places
> nor any second class people.

12   Home comer

But even so, he had to go home sometimes. For a rest, to see family and friends, to reconnect with his roots: for whatever reason, he came home. Yet we all know that time away often changes us, in ways which family and friends may not be expecting or even understand. When Jesus came home it was no different. Local people were not sure what to make of him. Even some family members were uncomprehending or hostile. Some hoped he would do in their village what he had done in other places. Others dismissed him as one might disregard anyone you have grown up with: what could be special about him?

Coming home

Now the day ends,
we are coming home:
relocating ourselves
after a day spent.

I locate myself in the Creator:
the awesome one of universal mystery.
I locate myself in the Companion:
the baptised one of universal company.
I locate myself in the Spirit
the advocate of universal peace.
I locate myself,
again and again and again
in the Holy Three.

As we come home,
to ourselves,
to each other
and to you, Home comer,
keep the vigil
with us this night
until we rise again,
ready to make a clean sweep
of the new day.

13   Story teller

Jesus came to change things. He made a difference in his community. The things he did changed the lives of others. He accomplished this in many ways but one was by teaching people – not in a classroom, but by using short stories from everyday life. Each story had a punch. They are called parables. A story about the seeds scattered in a field becomes a lesson about how much less there is to feed those who live on the margins of society. With these words Jesus reminded his hearers of their obligation to share fairly with those who had much less. But there are many other stories to remember and we can consider in what ways they feed us still.

Still growing

We are nurturing faith in each other:
listening or reflecting,
questions or stories.
Like well-worn farmers
we turn over the fertile soil.
With the tide falling,
like persistent waders,
we probe the exposed mud flats,
As wicket keepers
we stand ready to catch
the slippery stuff of life
as it slides into our hands.
We make little of it,
dismissing how these small acts
lubricate the life force.
Yet each of us knows
how hollow the feeling
when hounded on the empty shore
by the dogs of doubt.

14 Fishermen finder

The enormous lake which is the Sea of Galilee dominates the region. It is therefore not surprising that in an area where fishing was a major industry Jesus should meet some fishermen. It was a dangerous occupation then as now. The fishermen had probably heard about Jesus before he arrived on the lake shore. Maybe some of them had even seen him before. Rumours had been going round and for these fit young men he presented the obvious and only opportunity to escape their insular life of family and community. They wanted more than that, and by going with Jesus they certainly got more than they ever expected.

Fish for people

Our forebears were fish finders,
but these days there are few to find.
So we keep company with the Fish finder
and seek, with him, to fish for people.

15 Hillside teacher

Jesus did much of his teaching outdoors. As he travelled from place to place he would teach his followers. Whenever they stopped to rest, crowds would gather and he would give teachings. Galilee is a hilly place and this often happened on hillsides. Apart from storytelling, he would also use short sayings that might capture an idea, be easy to remember and create a puzzle to apply to life. Lots of these sayings survive, as do many suggestions about what they might mean. As a hillside teacher Jesus was not telling people what to think but how to think: how to keep on thinking and applying what he said to the situations they encountered every day. He invites us to continue to think about familiar words many times over in many different situations ... and to keep on thinking.

Truth sayer

Wild hills, mild hills
classrooms without walls;
as the clouds gather
and the curlew calls
we wait for the sun to sink
below our horizon
and recall today's lessons
from the Hillside teacher.

16 Enemy lover

Jesus lived in a country occupied by the Romans. Local people were
wary of the Roman army, and many feared and hated them
depending on their experiences. And after all, it is natural to hate
one's enemies – to hate them for the atrocities that happen near or far
away, the demands they make on the local community and economy,
for just being the enemy, for being different. Jesus' love extended even
to enemies. Anyone can love their friends, those they know well,
those with whom they feel safe and secure. It takes something else to
love the others, the different ones, the ones who sow suspicion and
fear inside us, the ones who have done wrong towards us.

Tough love

Jesus, remind us of what it takes to be your disciples.
When the going gets tough, it's not love for friends but enemies
that counts with you and marks us out as your followers.

17 Prayer instructor

In Jesus' day, a religious teacher would teach his people a prayer that they would learn by heart and share together. Today we know the prayer Jesus taught as the Lord's Prayer and it still serves the same function. We learn it by heart and we say it as a mark of who and whose we are. It's about all of life: the God we pray to and God's presence in the here and now as much as in eternity; the hereafter; the bread we eat each day and how we are tempted to keep it to ourselves, something only God can save us from. When Jesus teaches us to pray, he has everything covered, and as we pray this prayer we continue to learn from him.

> Encouraging tutor
>
> Teach us to pray
> every day.
> Teach us to breathe,
> to watch, to listen,
> to touch and taste
> the world around us.
> Teach us what to remember
> and how to forgive and forget.
> Teach us to encourage each other
> in this community.
> Teach us to pray
> every day.

18 Eye examiner

In a place where eye problems were common, it is not surprising that we find Jesus looking into a lot of people's eyes. Dusty, infected, tired and sore and some unseeing: such was the variety of eyes he examined. None of them could actually contain anything as big as a log. Another one of Jesus' jokes? Or true enough when we think about our own behaviour?

Any remembering about Jesus as Eye examiner may well link to stories of Jesus healing people with sight problems.

The whole picture

Just hold still a minute
Yes, I think that's got it.
Look, such a little speck.
Bet you feel much better now.

What do you mean, me?
What log? I can't see it.
You're having me on.
I can see.
I can see perfectly.

19 Sparrow sparer

Think of a sparrow. These small brown birds are common and virtually worthless. No one pays much attention to them except perhaps children with a few stale crumbs. But Jesus counts sparrows and claims that God does too. If God thinks so much of sparrows, then how much more does God think of you. There's a sketch about Jesus and sparrows on page 142.

20 Hair counter

Do you remember Jesus as Hair counter? Not only sparrows but hair counts with Jesus. Yet surely no one actually counts hair, do they? These are amongst many examples of the little things that Jesus talks up in his ministry, like yeast and mustard seeds. See what others you can remember.

Small stuff

The hair on your head,
the yeast in the flour,
the mustard seed in the palm of your hand;
all this counts with Jesus
and remember
you count too.

21 Seed sower

We might plough fields with tractors, but in those days everything was done by hand. Many people worked on the land but it was not often their land. They were labourers earning little enough. If they did own the land, most peasant farmers would have had just enough to live on, a precarious existence made more marginal by civic and religious taxes. Scattering seeds in a field means some seeds are bound to fall in less than ideal ground. When Jesus tells the story of the seed sower he is reminding folks about what they know. Furthermore, the worst yield in the most marginal soil was all the poorest people could expect to glean when harvest time came. What happens at the edges of the field may be an issue of life or death for some.

Soil samples

Seed sower,
remind us of your story in us.
Show us how to grow,

that our lives may bear fruit;
enough for everyone to live on.

Jesus often told stories about seeds. See if you can remember some others. There's another prayer about Jesus as seed sower called 'Sower, nurturer, winnower' on page 143.

22 Water walker

Whatever else he was, Jesus was a risk-taker. He took risks throughout his life. Life around the Sea of Galilee was risky. Water can be dangerous stuff, as anyone with a water-related job knows. Even doing water sports can be hazardous. But Jesus deliberately set out across a notorious stretch of water. So what does it take to be a risk-taker like this? A sense of adventure, self-confidence? It takes confidence in God's world and our place in it.

Media mania

It's a long time since we saw anyone walk on water.
Today's heroes can't do it;
celebrity lifestyle splashed across the tabloids;
documentary exposés, and world exclusives
sold for more than silver.
If it happened today, would the media just report
'Jesus of Nazareth cannot swim'?

23 Storm calmer

Storms were common on the Sea of Galilee. Its unique situation meant it had unpredictable weather patterns. Sensible fishermen and those with local knowledge would read the signs and avoid as best they could the most dangerous weather conditions. But sometimes they would be caught out and then it was everyone for himself to get to safe harbour. Jesus was asleep when the storm started, and quite

unaware, but even when woken by the others, the story tells us, he
was not afraid. Panic and fear, although natural, are not the most
useful responses in an emergency. Jesus took a no-nonsense approach
and the whole group came through the bad weather well enough to
remember this as a highly significant event. Such was his authority
that even the wind and waves seemed to obey him, something we'd
find difficult to replicate today. Stories like this are still well remembered by ordinary people even if they seem puzzling. What do they
say about Jesus – a man, or more than that?

Weather man

On a calm day it's easy to keep the horizon in sight,
not difficult to dream beyond it and keep up our spirits.
On a rough day even keeping our breakfast down is difficult
let alone lifting our heads up to see where you are calling.

24 People feeder

Feeding large crowds of people was one of the most memorable hall-marks of Jesus' ministry and frequently features in our remembered Bibles. There are several accounts of his doing this. Large crowds of relatively poor people would follow him around and eventually they would get hungry. His disciples were always a bit disorganised at this point, having made few if any arrangements in advance.

Hungry for change

It's all in your hands, People feeder:
the meeting and the eating,
the teaching and the learning,
the listening and the speaking,
the praying and the encouraging.
As we join hands to support and encourage each other,
may we know the hands we hold as your hands,
reaching out to these people and into this community.
As times change here, as everywhere,
may we see ourselves as co-workers with you,
feeding each other,
changing lives through this sharing.

25 Child blesser

In RB sessions, people frequently remember Jesus blessing the little children. Some rememberings will include rote recalled lines like 'Let the children come to me and do not try to stop them.' Even so, children and young people are still being marginalised in some Christian communities. How many times have you been told to 'keep quiet' during the service? How many people have scowled at our children in church? It seems we've still got quite a lot of work to do on this one.

Truly blessed

Bless the little children:
how many sugar-sweet pictures have you seen of that?
Yet childhood can leave a bitter taste
when abuse and secrecy dominate
and false relationships persist.
May those whose trust has been broken
find an oasis of truth and true communion
at the hands of the one who can really bless us.

26 Leper healer

People are still afraid of contagious illnesses, especially AIDS/HIV.
Leprosy was the AIDS/HIV of its day. Stigmatised and ostracised,
lepers were left out of everything, including the life of their own families and communities. No one would touch them. No one wanted
to be near them. Leprosy was a long, lingering death sentence. But
Jesus did not recoil from the lepers. His interaction with them shows
that overcoming superstition and fear are important in enabling
people to reclaim life in family and community. Challenging atti-
tudes like these is still part of restoring marginalised people to full
participation in life today.

'Christ makes with his friends a touching place ...'[31]

Touching

Touch me,
just touch me.
No one does,
no one dares.

One touch
is all it takes
to include,

to affirm,
to awaken.

Touch me,
just touch me.
Be the caring one,
be the daring one.

27 Rule breaker

There were several occasions when Jesus broke rules. These would
have been religious rules or social rules – things you were not supposed to do, particularly in relation to the Sabbath. Yet the Sabbath
itself was supposed to be a blessing to people and communities.
Whilst rules are important in community, it is also vital to get the
balance right. Too many rules can squeeze the juice out of life: the
energy, commitment and passion which make it flow. There is a
gospel story of Jesus responding to a question about Sabbath rules
which features a donkey in a ditch. If possible, always make space for
the odd quadruped when doing RB. It can lighten the load and provide the kind of running gag (pantomime-goers will know what I
mean) that can get you through even the most lengthy of sessions.
Some kind of donkey-related prop will help. I have an excellent
talking-donkey hobby horse given to me by some RN and RAF
chaplains which I often use for this purpose. Failing that, two people
in a donkey suit could also work well.

Donkey day

When donkeys fall in ditches
it's help that's needed, not rules.
When human beings are marginalised
or hurt by systems and regulations
help us to see beyond the legalisms
to full and abundant life for all your creatures.

28 Mind changer

There's an odd little incident when Jesus gets tangled up with a
woman, a Gentile and therefore an outsider, and her dogs. She
comes to see him about healing her daughter. He, wearily, rudely, at
first turns her away. But then the dogs get into the story: those under
the table, begging, snuffling, yapping, cursed and kicked. Even they
get the crumbs, it seems. Her answer makes Jesus see the situation
differently. One who will change many minds also has his mind
changed. The woman's child is healed and the crumbs are distributed
further.

Crumbs!

Only crumbs,
that's all it takes.
We who set the table now,
are we even aware of the dogs?
What notice do we take
of who gets the crumbs?
Mind changer,
change us.
Help us to see
that the broken bread
is not just for us.

29 Sin forgiver

The man whose friends raised the roof (see number 10 in this chapter on page 95) was not the only one to hear from Jesus, 'Your sins are forgiven.' What other encounters stick in your memory because of this affirmation? How has this phrase affected you and your discipleship?

Forgiving one

Christ, you bring us back,
from a place that few want to visit
but most of us inhabit from time to time.
You bring us back into community
with your simple phrase
and your accepting touch.
As we are released
may we release others.

30 Faith affirmer

For sins to be forgiven, don't you need faith? Jesus never seems to say how much faith is required beyond a tiny speck. Except when the centurion seeks healing for the unseen and unvisited servant. Jesus commends him – another foreigner and outsider – as having more faith than all the so-called faithful insiders.

Moving mountains

'Your faith has saved you.'
'How much faith was that?'
'About as much as a mustard seed.'
'What could that do?'
'It could move mountains.'

Faith affirmer,
only your company
can make me
a mountain mover.

31 Mountain climber

How many mountains did Jesus climb? (See page 52 for another RB mountain-based activity.) Climbing mountains is often seen as a sign of significant achievement. You might expect to get a good view unless the weather closes in. But it can also be dangerous. How do achievement and risk-taking feature in your remembering of Jesus as mountain climber?

Going up

On the way up I'm always pessimistic:
will I make it to the top?
When I get there, my lungs bursting,
there's something amazing
about seeing the world from on high.
Mountain climber,
help us to see the world your way.

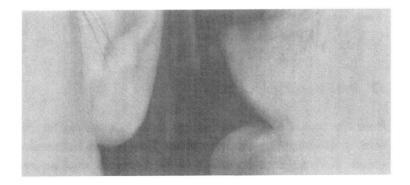

32 Spirit challenger

In the story of what happens at the bottom of the mountain, Jesus meets the family of a boy with epilepsy. In the language of his day this is described as having an evil spirit that stops the boy from speaking. As I've met more children with epilepsy and communication difficulties than I have with evil spirits, I tend to describe the boy using the language with which I am familiar.[32] Jesus explains the place of prayer in restoring a person's body, mind and spirit. There are other places in the gospels where Jesus is said to confront spirits of different kinds and to restore people to family and community. The place of prayer in the ministry of healing is also reaffirmed.

The way of prayer

Prayer makes the difference.
For every situation challenged;
for every person supported;
for every group reunited;
for every life put back on track;
always start with prayer.
Then continue in prayer,
uphold in prayer,
enfold in prayer.
Keep prayer central:
it's the vital way.

33 Road traveller

From the time of his baptism through to the last week of his life, what is remembered most often about Jesus is that he travelled around Galilee, Judea, Samaria and the Decapolis teaching and healing people as he went. He stayed in some places, of which a few are named; he met some people, many of whom remain anonymous.

There were actions, stories and conversations on the road. See what stories you can remember from Jesus' travels.

Desert days

Forty desert days and nights can seem endless.
It's okay for you and your macho desert friends,
practising your desert survival skills:
avoiding co-operating with the occupiers
by cohabiting with revolutionaries or holy fools.
You manage to make heat and dust look so easy,
surviving on what you can find,
but this is not the place
we all look forward to returning to
on an annual visit.
The desert may have its moments of beauty;
still star-filled nights, awesome vistas,
weather-etched outcrops
but as we enter the desert together again,
I wonder if we'll even find
the road to Jerusalem
on the other side.

34 Water drinker

Everyone needs water. Nowhere is this more obvious than in a hot country in the middle of the day beside a well. Jesus is unable to reach the water in the well and thereby quench his thirst. The woman who comes to the well at this unlikely time could get him some, but will she? You see, the woman and Jesus are from different groups that are traditionally suspicious of each other. They start to speak to each other, unlikely enough, but they seem to hit it off, and are soon talking about the really important things in life. With conversations like this, the woman feels satisfied. He seems to know so much about her. Will she ever be thirsty again?

Living water

A drink of water from the well woman was all you wanted.
It got you into one of those conversations that change life.
Now water is more than drink:
it flows, it satisfies,
it brings out the best in us.

35 Back straightener

Another way Jesus changed things for people he met was his
approach to those who were ill or disabled. In a society without
health care, sick or disabled people were generally shunned or iso-
lated due to fear or stigma. But Jesus didn't keep anyone at arm's
length. A woman who had not stood up straight for many years had
got used to being ignored and to looking at the ground. Jesus called
her Abraham's daughter and reinstated her as a full member of the
family – all the more amazing as Abraham was not remembered for
his daughters!

*These days back pain is the commonest cause of time off work among
British workers. How did this come about? What lies under the surface of
these untold stories?*

Back up

Straighten us out, Jesus.
Help us to face the world with our heads up:
to face the past and all that tries to break us;
to face the present and all that puts us under pressure;
to face the future so that we might bend like supple saplings
rather than be felled like broken beeches.

36 Tear shedder

When someone we love dies, grief is our common human response. Jesus demonstrated it in the shortest verse in the written Bible.* Like us, he cried at the death of his friend. Martha, Mary and Lazarus were friends he visited from time to time. He had been away for a while when he got news that Lazarus had died. Eventually he got back to their house where the two sisters were grief-stricken. A great crowd of people were also there so there was little privacy at this emotional time. When Jesus went to visit the grave he was visibly upset, just as any of us might be. Here he was at his most human.

* John 11:35

Sad but wise

What are you crying for?
Is it not enough that we can weep
without explanation;
as if words could express
every part of our humanity?
What are you crying for?
There's no need to spell it out;
it's enough that we cry
and share the ministry
of the Tear shedder.

Sad, wise God,
who in Jesus
wisely but sadly called Lazarus back to life,
call us back too,
that both wise and sad
we may make a new start
amongst your kin and kindom.[33]

37 Temple talker

Jesus talked in the temple from an early age. In the last week of his life he was still doing it. Speaking with authority marked him out from other religious leaders. What do people remember him saying in the temple or near it? What was his attitude towards the temple and what was happening there?

Stone marker

'Don't be fooled by stones, boys,'
he warned us on the way out.
'If these people were silent
then these stones would shout aloud.'
We who set such store by stones
need to be reminded of your temple talk.

A visit to the Manchester Science Museum

In the temple of science I sat by the turbulence dome: a globe full of shiny custard-coloured stuff which when it is spun round creates beautiful patterns like clouds skimming over a planet (Bob says it's Jupiter). Some children came and wanted it to go faster and another came and wanted it to go back-wards. And then a disabled child came up and watched the globe as it spun slowly. As it slowed down she tentatively put out her hand (a hand that had three fingers) and placed one finger gently on the surface of the globe. As I watched I thought, 'This is all we have to live on.'

38 Widow encourager

Knowing his society was one that often marginalised widows, Jesus made a point of encouraging them. One widow got a dead son back; another widow was commended for two mites. A dead husband might mean remarriage to his brother or another family member – security was hard to come by. How many widows do you remember Jesus encouraging and how?

Gone, but not forgotten

'It's a waste of time talking to me,' you said.
'You'd be better off talking to someone else.'
Down, down and deep down
it seems that your sense of worth dwindles and dies.
I kneel in front of you.
I take your hand.
I look at your face.
'But I'd like to talk to you.'
How else can I say
'I know the Life Giver. Do you?'

39 Donkey rider

When Jesus comes into the city on a donkey he is greeted by huge and excited crowds. Palm trees are stripped of their branches, cloaks are flung down to make a path. But being a donkey rider is not really celebrity status. Even if obscure prophets mentioned donkey riding as a sign of prophetic leadership, most people would not see this as the way of the red carpet.

Donkey rider

This is the week,
the week of cheers
that turn to mocking and jeers
and then to silence
that storms out of twisted streets
to stand at crossroads
in troubled cities across the world;
the half-remembered week
where guttering flames
and a few lined faces
keep this vigil, still;
the week that takes us further
than any other
and always ends in tears.

40 City weeper

Jesus weeps over the city where he will meet his death. It moves him
to see it laid out before him, to see the people and their struggles.

Dismal day

Weep, city, weep.
Weep, stones and streets,
houses and alleys:
weep now.
Weep with the Weeping One.
Who knows what makes for peace?
He knows and shows
the way to peace
for this and every city.

41 Tree curser

The bit where Jesus curses the fig tree is either highly memorable or easily forgotten. In a number of different rememberings of the Passion Week, some groups remember it many times and others forget it completely. It's an odd episode which seems out of character. What did this poor fig tree do to deserve this curse? Yet forever after the withered fig tree casts its shadow over the city.

Casting shadows

In a week of confusing encounters
from palm praises
to fig tree curses,
you move us relentlessly to a stark place
where only wood is left to speak
of pain and suffering, body and blood,
and we are left wondering about the meaning
of a simple tree.

42 Table turner

How many times did Jesus turn over the tables of the merchants in the temple? Depending on which written gospel you read, you might find it at the beginning or end of his ministry. But, like many events in the remembered gospel, perhaps we should think of him doing it more than once. How else would it stick in the memory so strongly? Maybe he did it on an early visit to the temple and then on a subsequent occasion saw that things were much as he'd encountered them the first time. Perhaps that made him angry again and over went the tables for at least a second time. Jesus is not often allowed to be angry (remember any other examples?) but his anger here is considered justified: pilgrims ripped off, commercial considerations instead of worship. So what about our own temples and houses of prayer: what's going on in those? Would it provoke Jesus' anger?

Prayerful prophet

Table maker,
familiar with furniture, its purpose and design;
you encourage our worship and prayer in the Maker.
Table turner,
angry at injustice and misdirected worship,
you call us to justice and true worship.
When our worship is bound up
with the position of furniture
more than the needs of the poor
help us to move on and change the world.

43   Commandment endorser

'Which commandment is the most important of all?' This could be
an important question if you live by commandments. You don't
want to choose the wrong one. The commandment to 'love God
with your whole being' would have been implanted in Jesus from an
early age.

In remembering commandments, remember also Jesus' new commandment: 'Love one another.'

Provoking choices

Companion Christ, chosen by you as friends,
appointed to be fruitful and enduring,
we place ourselves in your hands,
we commit ourselves to building your community.
May the lives we live be marked by whose we are
and whom we follow. [34]

44   Foot washer

'I remember Jesus washing his disciples' feet,' said one person to another one Maundy Thursday. 'Do you. Why did he do that?' said the other. And so began a conversation about the Foot washer.

In a dusty country, before sitting down to eat, it would be common to offer a bowl of water to wash hands and feet. Before Jesus and his disciples eat this last and most significant meal, Jesus starts to wash their feet. If they are surprised, only one voice is raised in protest: Peter's. He struggles with the notion that the one he sees as his leader, the one he looks up to, should stoop down and do such a lowly task. But Jesus was never afraid of dirt and seemed to have little regard for status.

Washing one

When we get to the stage
where someone has to wash us,
we fear the loss of dignity.
Even the able-bodied around this table
shunned this display of vulnerability
invited by the Foot washer.
Whether washed or washing,
may we live the moment
made new with water,
once more brought back to life.

45 Supper sharer

How many suppers did Jesus share and with whom? What about
those embarrassing ones, where several anonymous women poured
scented oil over his head or his feet or both? How many times did
that happen? If you think that these incidents happened more than
once, in more than one house, at more than one supper, it might
suggest a different meaning to the story than that of the one-off
deranged woman with more ointment than sense, who shows no
regard for the poor when she acts in poor taste. There might have
been several women whose insight into Jesus' ministry brought them
to this point of contact, despite the reaction they would receive.

> Remembering her
>
> Remember me:
> my ministry of anointing
> and the scandal it created?
> Remember me:
> my ministry rejected
> and my personhood negated?
> And remember my sisters
> who still seek to minister
> in the name of the Supper sharer.

46 Bread breaker

It was a simple meal and in sharing bread with his friends Jesus was
doing something that people still do today all around the world.
Bread is a basic foodstuff and he would have eaten it with his friends
on many occasions. On this night he blessed it and passed it round
with words that have travelled down the centuries: 'This is my body.
Do this to remember me.' Bread helps us to remember Jesus: one as
ordinary as ourselves, who ate bread. When we eat bread we
remember that he broke it and ate it and said this about it. Bread, the
stuff from which our bodies are made, is the stuff of his body.

At the blessing of the bread and wine ...

Hand shakes
Bread breaks
Dark cup
Lifted up
Poured out
Heaven's shout!

At the breaking of the bread ...

Disabled Christ,
your body was broken for us,
and in the heat of remembering
we proclaim your death and resurrection,
sharing together in suffering and rejoicing,
celebrating your everlasting way of love.

47 Garden pray-er

After this supper with his friends, Jesus goes to the Mount of Olives
and prays in the Garden of Gethsemane. Some disciples go with him,
including Peter, James and John. Jesus asks them to stay and pray with
him but after all the events of the week they fall asleep. Jesus himself
prays desperately, the stress of the situation showing both in his
prayers and in his response to his sleeping friends. He wakes them up
and the moment of betrayal arrives from out of the darkness.

Another garden

Once more to the garden,
once more into the night:
shadows and sleep confound
and prayer bites into your tongue.
Will we ever know this place?
Face the unnameable,

or pray the unspeakable?
For everyone who does face this
your unutterable company,
and everyone who might
your irrepressible presence.

48 Crown wearer

Having heard the charge that Jesus is claiming to be a king, his tor-
turers prepare a crown for him. It's all part of an agonising joke that
they play out, shouting 'Hail, King of the Jews,' as they push the
thorny crown down on his head. In some places where the Passion is
still publicly acted out, participants make crowns of actual thorns
and wear them as a sign of their identification with the crown wearer.

> Crown him
>
> An unwanted crown,
> an unasked-for title,
> an unimaginable agony.
> One more push,
> one more blow
> one more step.
> It is not yet finished.

49 Pain bearer

There's no getting away from the fact that Jesus' death was very
painful. The Romans chose crucifixion for the prolonged torture and
the agonising example it made of the victims. But pain is not to be
glamorised or sought out. Our responses to pain are understandably
universal. We want it to stop. Millions are spent annually on ways of
preventing pain (as well as on ways of creating it). In bearing pain,
Jesus is once more like us, and now even more vulnerable. The
means to stop the pain are not under his control. Now we get to the

heart of God. There are those who look at Jesus and say, 'How can this be God? Surely God would stop the pain.' Well some gods might, but not this one.

Creed

I believe I am like Jesus:
a human being,
birthed and breathing,
bouncing and kicking,
babbling brightly.
But bearing pain
is another matter.
From time to time
by disease, birth rite
or broken body part
a moment of solidarity
connects us again.
I believe I am like Jesus:
bearing pain,
one of the marks
of life before death.

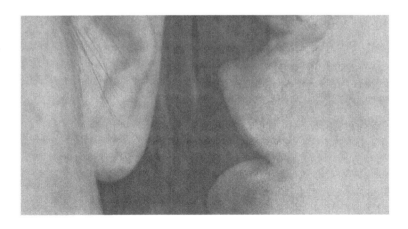

50 Torture forgiver

But pain inflicted by others in order to wield power is something quite different. We might squash a snail or swat a fly but which of us would inflict pain on another person? You only have to watch the news to get an answer to that.

And what about forgiveness: where does that fit in? 'Father forgive them, for they know not what they do' is one of the few rote-remembered phrases that regularly feature in RB sessions.

Here is a mesostic in the shape of a cross. Other patterns can be made from words or phrases from RB sessions.

```
                    F
                    a
                    t
                    h
                    e
                    r
  Father forgive
                    o
                    r
                    g
                    i
                    v
                    e
```

51 Death confronter

Jesus confronts death surrounded by women. The others have fled. The soldiers are gambling for his few possessions and only the women remain. Of those named, the obvious one is his mother. From his birth in a stable to his death on the cross she remains the constant presence. He commends her to the care of one of the few male disciples to remain behind. And it is she who, according to many artists, holds his dead body as it is brought down from the cross. We are embraced once again by the raw business of being human. Each of us waits for death in our own way, as did those participants at the cross.

Moving on

Not everyone knows the story of the empty tomb
and of those that do, not all of them believe it.
Approaching our own tombs we falter.
Standing on the edge of the tombs of those we love
we collapse inwards on ourselves,
memories stark, turning like knives.
It takes a patient story-crafter to listen
to the deep silences that well up through our fears.

Silent One, be with us.
Tomb quitter, be with us.
Story weaver, be with us.

Holy and inexhaustible Three,
be with us in our fear and in our passion,
as we live the story of your new life
and move on to the place of flourishing.

52 Stone mover

The tomb was cut out of rock and so it was sealed by an even bigger
rock, rolled across the entrance. No one was going to move this stone
easily. But then, just a few days later, it has been moved and the tomb
lies open. The women who have gone to the garden had wondered
how they would move the rock. They don't need to move it. It has
already been moved. So who moved it?

Stone roller

Roll that stone,
Roll that stone,
Roll that stone away.

53   Dawn gardener

In the early morning light, Mary of Magdala thinks she sees the gardener. Perhaps it's the kind of occupation best done early in the morning. She asks a question, not of the horticultural kind: 'Where is Jesus' body?' Although we know that when a person dies the body no longer holds the essence of their personhood, as human beings we still prefer to treat the dead bodies of those we love with reverence.

> 'Too early for the blackbird ...' [35]
>
> Early or late
> the blackbird is making a nest
> in the thickest part of the hedge:
> like a crown
> thorns surround the entrance.
>
> Early or late
> the blackbird is calling
> an alarm call across the garden:

naming the risk
greeting the possibilities.

Early or late
the blackbird watches the world,
for unlikely opportunities:
sheltering new life
she spies on us all.

Nest builder,
Risk namer,
World watcher:
now we see you,
now we don't.
May we early risers
or latecomers
recognise you and rejoice
in these glorious days.

54 Name caller

To be called names is generally viewed as a negative thing in our society. This is partly why I use this kenning here to describe Jesus. Part of what we are called to do is to renew our human understandings by viewing them in a new light. If Jesus is a name caller, what does that mean to us now?

Jesus calls Mary's name and that is how she recognises him. On other occasions he calls specific people by name: Simon Peter for example and Saul on the road to Damascus. But there are more encounters in the gospels with those not called by name which leave name calling as a bit of a mystery. Is it important or not? What do you make of it? Do you have a story of name calling to add to this?

Name calling

Companion Christ
we take your name with affection
calling you many names:
 Leper healer
 Supper sharer
 People feeder
 Cross carrier
 Power promiser.
We who welcome the morning
call you Dawn greeter,
to make our day into your day
with this sunrise.
Even so, come then, Jesus.

55 Tomb quitter

The tomb into which his body was placed just a few days previously is empty. Various people look inside to check this. It is, after all, difficult if not impossible to believe. There must be some explanation. The body stolen, hidden somewhere else – or perhaps he wasn't actually dead? Down the centuries countless people, both believers and doubters, have sought an explanation for this empty tomb. All we can do is look inside for ourselves and see it as they saw it. It is empty. Jesus is gone.

Among the dead

Whisper softly,
speak in hushed voices
but do not disturb the dying.
Be respectful,
keep your eyes lowered,
as death comes little by little.

But you,
you who have already been in the tomb
three or four days,
who have smelt your own stench
and then emerged
at the call of the Life Giver:
you are not afraid.

For you,
you who make up words
who use your own given name
and dance on graves
flinging bandages about
celebrating release:
you are not afraid.

You already know
that no body is here.
There's no point in seeking the living
among the dead.

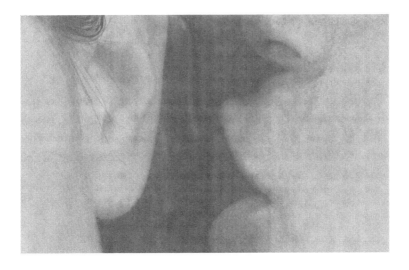

56   Onward traveller

Two friends meet a stranger on the road and try to explain to him what has been happening in recent days. He in turn explains to them what the hidden message is in all this chaos. They find themselves affected by his explanation and invite him to eat with them. The stranger was intending to go on somewhere else, but he stops briefly to eat with them. Once again, simple food is shared. Bread is broken and memories remake minds. Just as they realise the stranger's identity, he makes good his intention to travel on. They go back to the city to tell the others. We too must keep moving on.

Travelling on

At the threshold
you look as if you are going on.
They call you back.
You enter the house,
break the bread
and it all becomes clear.
But where were you going
when they interrupted you?
I'd love to know.

57   Wound bearer

Thomas has made it clear that he will only accept the risen Jesus if he is able to physically verify his presence. Only touching the wounds that he bears will be proof enough. These wounds are what, according to some disabled theologians, mark Jesus as one in solidarity with disabled people – the Disabled Christ.

'The buses run, it goes on raining'[36]

I don't have to see every bus
to know they are still running.
It doesn't have to rain every day
to know that rain still falls.
I don't have to touch every wound,
walk down every road,
taste every crust, drain every cup,
look into every eye to remember.
I don't have to cross every threshold
or hear every word to believe
that faith and doubt can live on.

58   Power promiser

What do people remember about Jesus' final words to his disciples?
This could be a good question with which to begin an RB session
about Jesus' Ascension. The disciples sense the end approaching but
they do not know the final day or hour. They receive Jesus' promise
of power, a promise to be with them, and us, to enable them to bap-
tise others and to share the gospel. This promise will last until 'the
end of the age'.

Send me

As I was sent
so you are sent.
Bless everyone
as God blesses you.

59   Footprint leaver

Story has it that at the place where Jesus went up to heaven, during
the event we call the Ascension, is a rock marked by two footprints.
Whatever these marks are, the idea that Jesus left us his footprints in
which ourselves to tread is what this series of reflections has been
about. Yes, he was remarkable, but he was also ordinary – as ordinary
as we are. If we are willing to reflect on the kind of life he led, on his
motives and actions, and consider him again as every day we try to
act as he would have done, then we are relating to Jesus as Footprint
leaver: one whom anyone can follow.

> Would you follow him?

> Would you follow him?
> Step into these footprints?
> Isn't it all just stuff for the gullible:
> water to wine, bread for body?
> Isn't it all too hazy
> like mist on a lake
> and tricks on the water?
> Isn't it all too twee
> with Good Samaritans
> and forgiven sons?
> Isn't it all too unlikely,
> like tiny seeds into massive trees,
> and a picnic for a multitude?
> Aren't there better explanations:
> a body stolen, an unreliable woman?

Yes, I'll follow him,
for all the possibility,
the could and might be,
the ordinary becoming extraordinary,
the wacky, the wobbly and the winsome.
Yes, I'll try the footprints.
Yes, I'll follow him
    as bread breaker,
    tomb quitter
    and life giver.

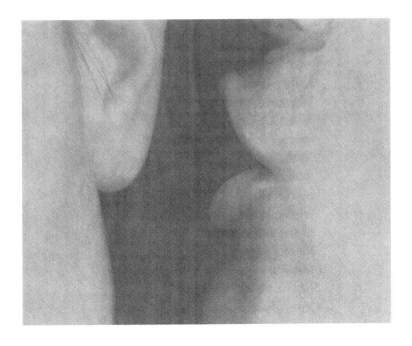

Taking the name

We are all like him:
born once
in a place we don't choose,
subjects of another empire.
Lost as children
by innate curiosity
or poor parenting.
Baptised as adults
by air, fire or water.
We wander,
collecting some,
discarding others,
teaching a few,
healing fewer.
We attend, more or less
to our bodies;
eating, drinking, remembering.
At the end
we die once
and for all,
hoping to rise
in love and memory
for fifty days
or more.
In vain we take the name:
Jesus Christ!

Are you the one?

Voice 1
Are you the expected one
or should we wait for someone else?
Should we get excited,
convert humanity,
establish the church
on the back of your story
or hang on for another?

Voice 2
If you are the one,
what is your relationship with the bigger one,
the Great Power?
Are you the Lesser One
the Little One?
Are you part of the Great One
or just a relative?

Voice 3
Were you there from the beginning
and if so why did you wait so long?
Why choose that time and place,
those followers and witnesses?

Voice 4
If you are the One
are you also one of us?
So much of what you did
we cannot do.
Huddled in our own tombs
we are not sure
if you are the one.
We've tried to feed the hungry
a bit;

Preach the good news
sometimes.

All
Is it enough?

Praise prayer[37]

Morning miracle maker
your song calls us to a new day
And we join with all who praise you.

Prediction defier
your presence unfolds a new sunrise
And we join with all who praise you.

Hope regenerator
your reflection awakens us to new possibilities
And we join with all who praise you.

Awesome and Holy Three,
this is the day:
    the day you have made;
    the day you quit the tomb;
    the day of your promise of power;
And we join with all who praise you.

What would Jesus say?

It was hot as usual, and dusty, and we were tired, as usual, hungry
and thirsty and fed up. We slumped on the grass.

He said, 'Blessed are the poor.'
And we said, 'Yeah, right. It's great to be poor, a real blessing,' and
picked our teeth.
And he said, 'The kingdom of heaven belongs to them.'
And we said, 'Much good might it do them,' and turned our backs.

He said, 'Blessed are those who mourn.'
And we said, 'Yeah, right. It's great to mourn. We all really enjoy
that,' and picked our toes.
And he said, 'They shall be comforted.'
And we said, 'Big deal,' and shuffled about.

He said, 'Blessed are the humble.'
And we said, 'Yeah, right. It's great to be humble:
doormats anonymous rule OK.'
And he said, 'They will receive what God has promised.'
And we said, 'Good luck to them,' and cleaned our fingernails.

He said, 'Blessed are those whose greatest desire is to do
what God requires.'
And we said, 'Yeah, right.' And couldn't think of anything else to
say, because we'd once thought that we too wanted to do what God
required, but now we were just like all the others – tired, dirty,
hungry and fed up.
And he said, 'God will satisfy them,' which from where we were
sitting didn't look too likely.

He said, 'Blessed are the merciful.'
And we said, 'Why the mercifcul?'
And he said, 'God will be merciful to them.'

And then we thought of all the times we'd struggled to show even
the smallest grain of mercy, and we shuffled about a bit more and
thought, 'This is all too hard.'

He said, 'Blessed are the pure in heart.'
And we said, 'Well, that counts us out,' and tried to ignore him.
And he said, 'They will see God,' which surprised us a bit so we
tried to take a bit more notice.

He said, 'Blessed are the peacemakers.'
And we said, 'Peacemakers eh? Who around here knows 'owt
about peacemaking?'
And he said, 'They will be called Children of God,' and we liked
the sound of that but it seemed a bit beyond us really.
And some other wags at the back of the crowd got hold of this one
and distorted it in a way that you'll have heard before and not forgotten, and who can blame them as he was going on a bit and we
were all hot, tired, hungry, thirsty and fed up.[38]

He said, 'Blessed are those who are persecuted because they do what
God requires.'
And we said, 'For goodness' sake, no one's going to want to do that,'
which just goes to show how far we'd come from those days of
leaving fishing boats and tax collecting and the like.
And he said, 'The kingdom of heaven belongs to them,' which was
an answer that always baffled us.

He said, 'Blessed are you when people insult you, and persecute
you, and tell lies against you because you are my followers.'
And we said, 'Well, this is more like it,' and remembered all the
things that had got us down recently, like being spat at, and getting
hungry, tired and fed up.

And he said, 'Be happy and be glad. There's a reward for you.'
And we said, 'Where?'
And he said, 'Ah, I thought that might make you sit up and take
notice. Where do you think it would be? Remember the prophets?
What happened to them? Well it's like that for you too.'
And we said, 'Great. Thanks.' And wondered why we'd come along
at all.

So he changed tack and said, 'You're like salt and light and yeast and
stuff like that.'
And we said, 'How come?'
And he said, 'Because even a tiny bit of those things makes a difference to people's lives. So, too, you will make a difference even if
now you feel useless, and worn out, and fed up. Even when you
think you're finished, God has not finished with you.'
And we said, 'It's stuff like this that keeps us hanging on in here
even when we're tired and hungry and fed up and don't really know
what you're going on about all of the time.'
And he said, 'Yeah, I know. Me too.'

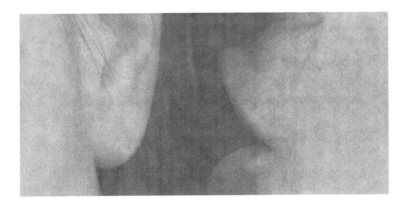

Creative activities with biblical images

There are biblical images that still crop up in enough conversations to suggest they are memorable. It's worth revisiting such images in a creative way and finding opportunities to translate them into contemporary encounters.

Those mentioned here include biblical images of animals. The two sparrows that are sold for a penny make a comeback as a sassy pair of birds who have something to say to us about our relationship to the environment. You could dress up the sparrows – perhaps make one weedy and tatty-looking and the other sparky and streetwise – but in any case these must be sparrows with attitude.

Sparrows

Two sparrows sitting in a hedge alongside a busy urban street:

'Here, are we really only worth a penny?'
'Yeah.'
'Explain to me why that lot out there are worth more?'
'Dunno.'
'Look at them, coming and going, throwing down rubbish …'
'Yeah.'
'Choking us with fumes, so we can't breathe …'
'Yeah.'
'Chopping down our hedges so we have nowhere to live …'
'Yeah'
'Killing off all the stuff we eat so we starve …'
'Yeah.'
'I wouldn't give a penny for any one of them.'
'No?'
'Mind you, if we become rare maybe the price of sparrows

will go up ...'
'Yeah.'
'And we'll be quids in!'
'Yeah?'

God of sparrows,
help us to listen to the world around us,
to learn the true worth of each small part
that together we may turn the world round.

Sower, nurturer, winnower

Glory to you, New Covenant Maker, sower of seeds,
for whom and through whom all things exist.
We thank you for recreating us.

Glory to you, Christ of the field, nurturer of seedlings,
pointing to the possibilities of growth.
We thank you for being with us.

Glory to you, Harvesting Spirit, winnower of husk and chaff,
blowing through our hopes for today.
We thank you for renewing us.

Glory to you, Holy Three, wholly one,
dancing together like thistledown on the wind.
We dance with you and celebrate your gift of life.

Quitting the tomb [39]

I am always reluctant to go back. Even when someone I know well asks me, I hope they'll find someone else to take them – one of the others who was also there. Of course it's never the same, not like that first morning, although it takes me back to that day, at least partly. In the early days the memories were more vivid. The hairs on the back of my neck would stand up from the moment I set foot in the garden. I'd remember the smell of the earth and the call of the blackbird.

I have been back on several occasions, although less and less frequently. The birds still sing but the tomb is empty. And that is really at the heart of my reluctance to retrace the path to that place. Once I'd seen it was empty the first time, I didn't need to keep looking. Of course I accept that others didn't have the same encounter, didn't hear him call their name in the half light. But I did tell them what he said.

I wasn't the only one he spoke to. That helped because clearly we couldn't all have made it up. Mary and Cleopas were most compelling when they told us of the companion they met on the road, the storytelling and the bread-breaking.

And I can see that the tomb could be something of a magnet, containing as it does so many unanswered questions for us all. Why did it end like that, if indeed it has ever ended at all? I can understand the need to look inside, for each person to see the evidence for themselves, to wonder.

It has been many years now since I first saw it was empty. I have thought about it for most of my life. I've told the story of the empty tomb and other stories, woven out of the daily encounters we had on the road, and which still go on around me today. I try to emphasise how close he is to us now, how the stories he told are relevant to us today, how their equivalent can be found in the stuff of our daily lives.

Sometimes there is a positive response, like a spark catching hold of dry wood, or a seedling pushing its first leaves into the sunlight. It is not an easy story to tell. To truly tell it you must live it, believing each day will be an opportunity for a life-changing encounter. Perhaps that is why he chose me, because he knew I would go on doing that, come what may.

I've been doing it since that first morning, perhaps even before then. I will carry on doing it as I follow the road ahead. Leave the tomb: it is empty.

> *'Leave the tomb,' the angels said,*
> *pointing the way to the exit*
> *like cinema usherettes.*
> *'He's gone to Galilee,' they said,*
> *urging the women onwards.*
> *'Tell the others.'*
> *I did but not all of them believed me.*

How to use this story
This story is good for Easter Day or the weeks between Easter and Pentecost. Try to tell it in your own words rather than read it out.

Blessing

May Mary's God bless you.
May the Life Giver keep you company.
May the Spirit show you direction.
May the Holy Three watch, keep and sustain you
now and always.

NOTES

29 The Feast Day of the Massacre of the Innocents is observed around 28th December, depending on whether you are 'east' or 'west'.

30 There have been a number of desert conflicts in the last few decades. This was written after the 2003 invasion of Iraq.

31 A line from the song 'Christ's is the world in which we move' by John L. Bell and Graham Maule, number 724 in *Church Hymnary 4*.

[32] There's more on this story in *Word of Mouth*, pages 109-112.

[33] I often use the word 'kindom' to indicate a gender equal community.

[34] Written for Vision4life Prayer Year for use at the United Reformed Church General Assembly, Loughborough, July 2010.

[35] This is the first line of a hymn by Caryl Micklem. It is number 249 in *Rejoice and Sing*.

[36] This title is taken from a review of the book *The Goldhawk Variations* by Brian Louise Pearce (1999). He died aged 72 in April 2006 around Easter. He was a member of Twickenham United Reformed Church.

[37] CWM Europe Evangelism meeting in Cardiff, January 2010.

[38] You might recall this well known piece of RB from the Monty Python film *The Life of Brian*.

[39] Scotland, 22.02.2007

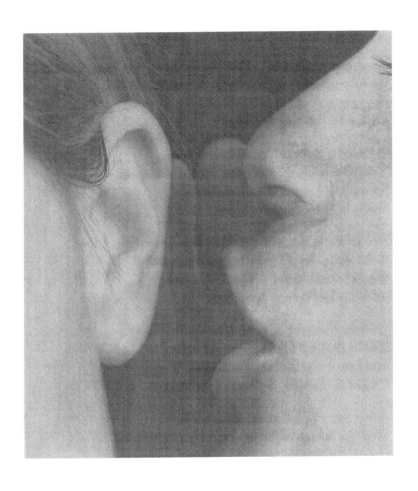

Appendix

Words for *Tell Me the Stories of Jesus*

These two versions of *Tell Me the Stories of Jesus* from either side of
the Atlantic are thought to be in the public domain.

Version 1 by William H Parker

Tell me the stories of Jesus I love to hear;
Things I would ask Him to tell me if He were here;
Scenes by the wayside, tales of the sea,
Stories of Jesus, tell them to me.

First let me hear how the children stood round His knee,
And I shall fancy His blessing resting on me;
Words full of kindness, deeds full of grace,
All in the love light of Jesus' face.

Tell me, in accents of wonder, how rolled the sea,
Tossing the boat in a tempest on Galilee;
And how the Maker, ready and kind,
Chided the billows, and hushed the wind.

Into the city I'd follow the children's band,
Waving a branch of the palm tree high in my hand.
One of His heralds, yes, I would sing
Loudest hosannas, 'Jesus is King!'

Show me that scene in the garden, of bitter pain.
Show me the cross where my Saviour for me was slain.
Sad ones or bright ones, so that they be
Stories of Jesus, tell them to me.

Version 2 words by Fanny Crosby

Tell me the story of Jesus,
Write on my heart every word.
Tell me the story most precious,
Sweetest that ever was heard.
Tell how the angels in chorus,
Sang as they welcomed His birth.
'Glory to God in the highest!
Peace and good tidings to earth.'

Refrain
Tell me the story of Jesus,
Write on my heart every word.
Tell me the story most precious,
Sweetest that ever was heard.

Fasting alone in the desert,
Tell of the days that are past.
How for our sins He was tempted,
Yet was triumphant at last.
Tell of the years of His labour,
Tell of the sorrow He bore.
He was despised and afflicted,
Homeless, rejected and poor.

Refrain

Tell of the cross where they nailed Him,
Writhing in anguish and pain.
Tell of the grave where they laid Him,
Tell how He liveth again.
Love in that story so tender,
Clearer than ever I see.
Stay, let me weep while you whisper,
Love paid the ransom for me.

Refrain

Bibliography

The following books have helped in the writing of this book:

Barker, GA, and Gregg, SE (2010) *Jesus, Beyond Christianity: The classic texts*. Oxford: Oxford University Press.

Bauckham, R (2006) *Jesus and the Eyewitnesses: The gospels as eyewitness testimony*. Cambridge: WB Eerdmans.

Beavis, MA (2002) (ed) *The Lost Coin: Parables of women, work and wisdom*. London: Sheffield Academic Press.

Borg, M and Crossan JD (2008) *The Last Week: What the Gospels really teach about Jesus' final days in Jerusalem*. London: SPCK.

Croft, S, et al (2005) *Evangelism in a Spiritual Age: Communicating faith in a changing culture*. London: Church House Publishing.

Davie, G (2007) *Sociology of Religion*. London: Sage.

Davis, J (2005) *Sacred Art*. Norwich: Jarrold Publishing.

Delloye, M (2009) *Le Rythme de L'Âne: Petit homage aux baudets, grisons and autres bourricots*. Paris: Transboreal.

Fisher, L (2003) *Will You Follow Me? Exploring the Gospel of Mark*. Edinburgh: Scottish Christian Press.

Funk RW and the Jesus Seminar (1999) *The Gospel of Jesus According to the Jesus Seminar*. Santa Rosa: Polebridge Press.

Steven Galloway (2008) *The Cellist of Sarajevo*. London: Atlantic Books.

Glasson, B (2006) *I Am Somewhere Else: Gospel reflections from an emerging church*. London: Darton, Longman and Todd

Harpur, J (2007) *The Gospel of Joseph of Arimathea*. Glasgow: Wild Goose.

Horwath, J; Lees, J; Sidebotham, P; Higgins, J and Imtiaz, I (2008). *Religious parents just want what's best for their children: Religion, belief and parenting practices, a descriptive study*. London: Joseph Rowntree Foundation.

Herzog, WR (1994) *Parables as Subversive Speech: Jesus as pedagogue of the oppressed*. New York: John Knox Press

Herzog, WR (2005) *Prophet and Teacher: An introduction to the historical Jesus*. New York: John Knox Press

Kendall, DR (2002) *Allegories of Heaven: An artist explores the 'Greatest Story Ever Told'*. Carlisle: Piquant.

Lees, J (2007). *Word of Mouth: Using the remembered Bible for building community*. Glasgow: Wild Goose.

Lees, J (2007). 'Remembering the bible as a critical pedagogy of the oppressed.' In GO West (ed) *Reading Other-wise: Socially engaged biblical scholars reading with their local communities*. Atlanta: Society for Biblical Literature.

Lees, J (2007). 'Enabling the body.' In H Avalos; SJ Melcher and J Schipper (eds). *This Abled Body: Rethinking the Bible and disability studies*. Atlanta: Society for the Study of Biblical Literature.

Lees, J (2009) *Hearing what parents say about children learning to talk*. Unpublished PhD Thesis, University of Sheffield.

Paynter, N and Coleman, D (2007) *Iona, Images and Reflections*. Glasgow: Wild Goose.

Polhill, C (2006) *A Pilgrim's Guide to Iona Abbey*. Glasgow: Wild Goose.

Perrin, N (2007) *Thomas: The other gospel.* SPCK.

Pullman, P (2010) *The Good Man Jesus and the Scoundrel Christ.* London: Canongate

Sample, T (1994) *Ministry in an Oral Culture: Living with Will Rogers, Uncle Remus and Minnie Pearl.* Louisville: Westminster/John Knox Press.

Slee, N (2004). *Women's Faith Development: Patterns and processes.* Aldershot: Ashgate.

Soskice, J (2009) *Sisters of Sinai: How two lady adventurers found the hidden gospels.* London: Chatto and Windus.

Thatcher, T (2006) *Jesus the Riddler.* New York: John Knox Press.

Thatcher, T (2008) (ed) *Jesus, the Voice, and the Text: Beyond the oral and the written Gospel.* Waco, Texas: Baylor University Press.

Toulson, S (1985) *Celtic Journeys in Scotland and the North of England.* London: Harper Collins (Fount).

Vickers, S (2006) *The Other side of You.* London: Fourth Estate.

West, GO (1999). *The Academy of the Poor: Towards a dialogical reading of the Bible.* Sheffield: Sheffield Academic Press.

West, GO (2007) (ed). *Reading Other-wise: Socially engaged biblical scholars reading with their local communities.* Atlanta: Society for Biblical Literature.

About the author

Janet Lees is
- a speech therapist with 30 years' experience of working with children with communication difficulties and their families;
- a minister of the United Reformed Church, having worked in pastorates in Twickenham and Sheffield; currently Co-ordinator of the United Reformed Church's Vision4life process and Chaplain at Silcoates School, Wakefield;
- a researcher who has studied religious families in Yorkshire.
- a writer with extensive publications in human communication, disability, parenting, women in the church and contextual Bible study;
- a human being married to Bob Warwicker and mother to Hannah Warwicker; she lives in Huddersfield, West Yorkshire.

Index